Making Marriage Work

Exploring Secrets Of Success In Marriage

Faith A. Oyedepo

MAKING MARRIAGE WORK

Copyright © 1997 by:
Faith A. Oyedepo

Reprinted in 2015

Re-edited : 2013

ISBN 978-2480-76-2

Published in Nigeria by:
DOMINION PUBLISHING HOUSE

For further information or permission, write:
DOMINION PUBLISHING HOUSE
Faith Tabernacle, Km 10, Idiroko Road, Canaanland, Ota.
P.M.B. 21688, Ikeja, Lagos, Nigeria.
Tel: 234-1-7747546-8

Web: www.davidoyedepo.org ; www.faithoyedepo.org

E-mail: dph@davidoyedepoministries.org

All scripture quotations are from the King James Version of
the Bible, except otherwise stated.

CONTENTS

Dedication

This book is dedicated to all, who desire to make their marriages work through the application of God's Word.

Introduction

Right from creation, God demonstrated His interest in and value placed, on the marriage institution and the family, by being practically involved in its institution. He did not simply speak it into being, as He did the beast of the field and the fowls of the air. He carefully put it together step by step.

God put man to sleep and from his side took a rib and formed the woman. Not stopping there, God took the woman by the hand and led her to Adam. Therefore, marriage is a unique relationship, having its root in divinity (Genesis 2:22).

However, marriage and family life, a thing of joy, pleasure and high esteem at creation, is now treated by many, as a necessary evil and looked at by some disdainfully. "Those in it want to rush out and those outside want to rush in," they say. This has resulted in the fast disintegration of the marriage unit and subsequently the family.

Statistics indicate that the **decline** of marriage and the family unit has been greater and more alarming in the past 25 years, than during any other quarter century in history!

These are pressure- filled times for the world and for the family unit in particular, all of which of course are in line with Biblical prophecies. The prophets of old foresaw that with the close of the age, there would be an ever-increasing breakdown of moral standards, with marriage and the family, being the primary target of the arsenals of the enemy.

> *...In the latter times some shall depart from the faith...having their conscience seared...forbidding to marry...*
>
> 1 Timothy 4:1-3

The spirit of rebellion, defiance and subsequently shame have taken hold of young people, causing them to rebel against all recognized authority (2 Timothy 3:1-3).

God has a purpose for marriage and until that purpose is discovered and applied, it does not produce fulfilment. For further reading on God's concepts for marriage, marriage as a covenant and a step-by-step analysis of the purpose for marriage, read my book, **Marriage Covenant**.

Your marriage and family life are meant to bring you tremendous joy. But not all couples are enjoying their

6

marriages. In fact, many are facing constant crisis and terrible difficulties and God is not unaware of this. That is why He inspired me to write this book.

In this book therefore, we will explore the subject of marriage and see that it can work, just as God designed it to, bringing honour, pleasure and satisfaction.

The excellent taste of every soup is determined by how it is prepared. It is not enough to have all the required ingredients, you must know how to correctly put them together, before you can get the desired taste. The same is true for marriage. What your marriage turns out to be, depends on how you make it. It is, therefore, your responsibility to make it work!

In this most exciting book, you will discover how. Let's get started!

1

Marriage Is Good!

Marriage is a union. It is the coming together of two people of opposite sex, with a view to building a God-centred home. One man, one woman. It involves a higher level of relationship with each other, than with any other person on earth. It is a union of spirit, soul and body (Genesis 2:24).

When a man and a woman come together as husband and wife, they are expected to have entered a better way of living. Ecclesiastes 4:9 says:

Two are better than one; because they have a good reward for their labour. Two are better than one; because they have a good reward for their labour.

The woman becomes the responsibility of the man. She is catered for, cherished and nourished by him. The husband brings in the material things, while she puts them together, making their home a place of glory. Both of them put in their time, strength, money, etc, to ensure that their home is built.

When a home is not founded upon God, the joy, excitement and satisfaction the couple had at the outset are short-lived. They soon wear off. It's like owning a car. With time, new models come out and what was once new begins to age. The car owner now desires to change the once new car for the latest sensation. Why? This is because the old one does not excite him anymore.

However, when God is at the centre of a marriage, you find that instead of getting tired of each other, your excitement and satisfaction increase as the years go by, making the relationship go from good to better and from better to best!

Marriage is good! Don't think that marriage is for shame and reproach. No, my friend! You don't have to settle for an average home, you don't have to put up with continuous quarrelling and fighting; you can make that marriage work! You can have a marriage free of hurts and wounds, you can enjoy fulfilment and God's goodness.

That is the realm of marriage God wants you to enter into. He wants to bring you to a point where men and even devils are compelled to acknowledge God's glory that is all over your family. That is your heritage as a child of God!

Benefits Of Marriage

God designed marriage to involve the spirit, soul and body, so that the blessings marriage carries is expected to affect your spirit, soul and body. When God blesses the union of a man and woman, certain things follow.

Spiritual Strength

God expects the married couple to become stronger spiritually than when they were both single. Two of them brought together in warfare against the devil, will cause 10,000 devils to flee (Deuteronomy 32:30). They thus become a greater terror to the devil than they were before marriage.

However, many people (women in particular) complain of not being as spiritually active as they were before marriage. Some claim it is because they are faced with greater responsibilities (a husband and children to look after, meals to cook, and general household chores), particularly if they are also employed outside the home.

However, this does not negate God's Word which declares that, "**Two are better than one**" (Ecclesiastes 4:9). The blessing of a husband and children should not be used as an excuse not to stay in touch with God; otherwise, you are opening up for the blessing to be turned into a curse. All you need to do is believe

11

God for better time management, so that nothing suffers — neither your walk with God nor your family (Ephesians 5:15-16).

Prayer Power

Marriage offers the couple unity, so that when they offer prayers to God on any issue at all, He honours their request. Why?

> *...If two of you shall agree on earth as touching any thing that they shall ask, it shall be done for them of my Father which is in heaven.*

Matthew 18:19

A couple is more readily united on issues than any two friends. For instance, if they require the fruit of the womb, and both of them believe God for it, not wavering, God is compelled to grant their request. Thus, when a man and his wife agree, there is tremendous power released; and if they disagree, their prayers are hindered (1 Peter 3:7).

Divine Favour

Another benefit of marriage is His divine favour.

> *Whoso findeth a wife findeth a good thing, and obtaineth favour of the Lord.*

Proverbs 18:22

Once this favour is present, it is irreversible. Even men are compelled to favour you, because when a man's ways please the Lord, He causes even his enemies to be at peace with him. The favour of God elevates you to such great heights that men begin to envy you. You become a reference point of a good marriage. When you step out, hand in hand with your partner, people will begin to whisper, "See those two, you would think they only got married yesterday." Marriage then becomes desirous, which is what it should be.

God's favour also secures for you a lifting and promotion in status, often occurring in an increase in material possessions, finances, etc.

Taking a look at the first family (Adam and Eve), one discovers that even after the fall, Adam's family still enjoyed God's favour. They had sewed fig leaves together and made aprons to cover their nakedness. But because of the special favour God reserved for the family, God overlooked their betrayal and clothed them with animal skin. He clothed their nakedness and thus removed shame from them.

In spite of the fact that Eve was the one deceived and the primary cause of the fall, out of favour, God made her a promise in Genesis 3:15:

And I will put enmity between thee and the woman,

and between thy seed and her seed; it shall bruise thy head, and thou shalt bruise his heel.

Companionship

Iron sharpeneth iron; so a man sharpeneth the countenance of his friend.

Proverbs 27:17

Husband and wife will enjoy greater light, when they put heads together to make decisions affecting their family.

For instance, there are some decisions I would have taken that would not have profited me; but because I'm privileged to be married to my husband, a man of integrity, who is sincere and godly, those errors were avoided. Several times, we would sit down to discuss issues that affect our family and the results always amaze me. Why? Simply because God has made provisions for **iron to sharpen iron** within the union.

However, there's no way two pieces of iron can sharpen each other, except they both come together in contact. Thus, this provision only works when you are united as a couple.

Finally, be ye all of one mind ...

1 Peter 3:8

Friend, you can tap into the honour God has reserved

for those united in purpose. But the problem with many families and the reason nothing seems to be working is that, many times, both parties have not caught the same picture of their desire. They are not united in purpose, so they slow down their blessings from coming.

Imagine what would have happened to the tower of Babel, if someone had said, "Let's use cement blocks", and the other had said, "No, let's use stones", and yet another, "Let's use bricks." They may still have been there arguing till today! You need to apply this spiritual principle of agreement to see your dreams come true.

Divine Security

> *...If one prevail against him, two shall withstand him; and a threefold cord is not quickly broken.*
>
> Ecclesiastes 4:12

God, the husband and wife form a three-fold cord that is not quickly broken. As man co-operates with God and establishes God's purpose for marriage in the home, God honours that family by ensuring that nothing prevails against it. They (the man and his wife) are equipped to withstand, with the help of the Lord, all demonic forces and the pressures of the secular world.

Physical Fulfilment

God honours the physical union of a man and his wife, by ensuring that they find pleasure and fulfilment in each other's body. Apart from preventing temptation, both husband and wife satisfy their sexual urge. They are provided with legitimate avenues to release their sexual desires.

This is why God frowns at adultery, because your partner should be enough to satisfy you. I often say humorously, that there is nothing another man or woman has that your partner doesn't have. All you need is to be content with your spouse, then you will enjoy the blessings of marriage.

Fruit Of The Womb

> *...They have a good reward for their labour.*
>
> Ecclesiastes 4:9

One of such rewards is the fruit of the womb.

> *Lo, children are an heritage of the Lord: and the fruit of the womb is his reward.*
>
> *Psalm 127:3*

The marriage union is expected to produce children. That was God's plan from the beginning (Genesis 1:26-28). If it doesn't, grief and frustration often set in.

The fall of Adam and Eve was what opened the door to barrenness. But God sent Jesus to redeem mankind from every curse of the law. Now, if you are born again, you are exempted from barrenness! Therefore, see your griefs and frustrations ending right now. Children are your entitlement if you are serving the Lord.

However, the seal of God's approval is not in just having children, but raising godly ones! At school, children are pressured into drugs, homosexuality and premarital sex. But when they have a solid Christian family to fall back on, they are able to withstand the lure of those things.

Divine Presence

...If two lie together, then they have heat...
Ecclesiastes 4:11

The enemy is walking to and fro looking for "cold" homes to infiltrate. When there's fighting, discord, selfishness, quarrelling, and unforgiveness, the home can be said to be "cold". But when there is love, understanding and harmony in a home, God rewards it with the warmth of His presence and peace that burns off the attacks of the devil, which could cause tension. For in His presence is fullness of joy and pleasures (Psalm 16:11).

Although God ensures His presence and peace, the

man and his wife still have the responsibility to lie together to enjoy it. That means God's presence is guaranteed, when the husband and wife join hands together to ensure that their marriage is run according to God's prescriptions, such as unconditional love from the husband and submission by the wife and doing other little things to keep the family "aflame".

The man and his wife must keep adding "wood" to their home, to ensure that the fire there never goes out (Proverbs 26:20).

Lifting By Men

It is an established fact that even the human society honours the married. For instance, once you are married, you are entitled to certain jobs and key positions because you are regarded as being responsible. Even if a woman is a young girl of about 20, the mere fact that she is married earns her respect and certain benefits. In spiritual settings also, there are certain key offices that only the married can occupy.

You Never Fall

For if they fall, the one will lift up his fellow...
Ecclesiastes 4:10

Whenever any party in a marriage relationship is weak,

the other can lift him up by strengthening him. The stronger can pray, declaring God's Word, thus raising up the weak or falling spouse. I remember a time when my health was being attacked. I had prayed, declared the Word and did all I knew to do; but nothing seemed to be working. But then my husband received an insight from God's Word, prayed over me and that ended the trial! I was healed and delivered!

Marriage is God's strategy to ensure that you never fall into depression and loneliness, away from the faith, into error, or fall a victim of any of the strategies of the devil.

Protection From Enemies

The story of Esau and Jacob readily comes to mind here. Esau, who had felt cheated out of his birthright and sworn revenge, suddenly had a change of heart towards Jacob. Apart from this being attributed to the intervention of God, I believe a tool God used to soften Esau's heart was his seeing Jacob's wives and children.

> *... Esau ran to meet him and embraced him...And he lifted up his eyes, and saw the women and the children...*

Genesis 33:4-5.

Respect from man is not only obtainable when they

like you. Even if they are adversaries, simply because you are in God's kind of marriage, they are compelled to honour you! That was what happened in the case of Abimelech, who had to honour Abraham when he discovered that Sarah was his wife. As compensation, he offered Abraham his land to dwell in as he pleased. He also gave him a thousand pieces of silver (Genesis 20:15-16).

All through their sojourn in the land of Canaan, no one could harm or treat Sarah wrongly because she was Abraham's wife. They respected her. Can you imagine what may have happened to her if she were not married?

How Do You See Marriage?

God designed marriage to work, but how you see it will determine whether it works for you or not. You must agree with God that when you enter into holy matrimony, you are stepping into a better way of life. Many lack this understanding, so they don't enjoy the benefits of marriage.

Marriage is good, it is precious by God's design. But God works in collaboration with His children, to establish His will on the earth.

Therefore, you must know and understand that there is profit for you in marriage, and this understanding will enable you to make the most of it.

Man that is in honour, and understandeth not, is like the beast that perish.

Psalm 49:20

Any marriage outside Christ cannot escape difficulties and troubles. No wonder, married unbelievers see themselves as trapped. If you are not born again, you are not entitled to the fulfilment in marriage that God has reserved for those who love Him. But God's grace is extending towards you right now; that grace is the carrier of salvation.

If you respond to it today, you will escape the distress the world is facing. If you desire right now to be born again, say this prayer of faith with me:

"Dear Lord Jesus, I accept that I am a sinner worthy of death. But I now understand that by inviting You into my life, I will be pardoned of all my sins. Forgive me of my sins and come into my heart right now. Take my life Lord and mould it. I turn my back on Satan and the world. Thank You for coming into my heart, in Jesus' name. Amen."

2

The Pillar Of Love

One major requirement for making your marriage work is love. Love here is not optional, but mandatory. This love does not have its origin in the world, but in God; for as God's Word declares, "God is love" (1 John. 4:8).

Husbands, love your wives, even as Christ also loved the church, and gave himself for it.

Ephesians 5:25

God, through Apostle Paul, issued this commandment to all husbands. It is not an admonition or suggestion, but an instruction that must be obeyed. God makes it mandatory for husbands to love their wives, sacrificially and unconditionally. You may argue that it is easy for me to talk, not knowing your wife's character. But let me remind you that your wife's nature notwithstanding, God expects you to love her. After all, while taking your marriage vows, you willingly said before all witnesses that you would love her.

Until you love your wife as Christ loves His Church, you are not walking in agreement with the Word of God. Christ's love for His Church is not only when she obeys Him, but even when she offends also (Romans 5:8). God's Word instructs you to love your wife in spite of her shortcomings. Until you comply with this commandment, you may never taste fulfilment in the family. You must ask God to rekindle the love for your wife in your heart. Particularly, according to God's Word, the love for one's wife must come after the love of God (Ephesians 5:28-29).

Your love for your wife must be expressed. I read an inscription on a wall some years ago which said, "Love is not love until it is expressed." This is true! God gave His love expression; you also must give your love expression.

How can love between husband and wife in particular, and family members generally, be expressed? This can be done in thoughts, words and actions.

Loving In Thoughts

Love is essentially a matter of the heart that eventually finds expression through the mouth and by actions.

Husbands must learn, beginning from the thoughts of their hearts, to love their wives. Out of the abundance of the heart the mouth speaks (Matthew 12:34).

When your heart is full of loving thoughts, it readily finds expression in the words you speak. If a man for instance, uses abusive words on his wife, he is speaking out of the abundance of his heart. Until he sees the content of his thoughts, he cannot speak otherwise.

Men initiate things and women respond to them. Husband, initiate the love relationship between you and your wife and she will respond to you. No woman hates to be loved.

When you love your wife, you easily win her submission.

Loving In Words

"I love you." Three short words, yet by them men and women come together to establish God's counsel on the earth. Often, however, these words are forgotten after the euphoria of the wedding ceremony is over.

Words are powerful and saying, "I love you" over and over again, spices up the marriage. Just like it is necessary for rain to fall again and again for farmers to reap a bountiful harvest, so also is it necessary to say "I love you" over and over again.

The relationship started off by the use of these three words and should grow also by its continuous use. The presumptuous claim that it's not necessary to say it over and over again because, "She should know I love her," is wrong. The Bible points out the importance of voicing out what one believes in the heart (Romans 10:10).

What you believe in your heart, you need to say with your mouth. No one can read minds, and until thoughts are voiced they remain private.

Faith, the Bible tells us, comes by hearing. If faith, the all- important mountain mover, becomes ours by the simple act of hearing, imagine how many mountains will be moved out of your homes when you say "I love you" to your spouse often!

Give voice to your feelings, it is not foolishness! The world was made by faith-filled words. Let your "I love you" to your spouse be full of faith. Even if your spouse is a monster, she would be changed to a marvel!

That's how God won man to Himself — while we were yet sinners, Christ died for us, thus saying "I love you" to people who rejected His love.

Husband and wife must learn to speak kind words to each other. Words create the right atmosphere in your home. Express to your mate the nice qualities you like in him or her.

Husband, handle your wife with care by speaking kind

words of appreciation to her often. She needs to hear you express daily how much you love and appreciate her.

Wife, don't nag your husband to death by repeatedly pointing out his shortcomings or problems in your home. Where there is a need for correction, use the sandwich method— compliment, correct and then compliment.

Compliments

Praise your spouse for doing something well or for something you like about him or her. Everyone loves to be praised, everyone loves nice things to be said about them. It is giving flesh to "I love you".

Men and women who are not complimented, do not feel appreciated. They feel taken for granted and ordinary. So, when someone outside showers them with the much sought for compliments, they are easily taken captive.

Let's do our homework. Appreciating little things creates greater things. Nothing should escape our praise; it motivates the beneficiary to go a step further. When a wife hears "I love you" from the husband, her countenance changes. She cannot hear too much of it. My husband is never too tired to appreciate and say "I love you" to me. Each time I hear that from him, I'm excited and on top throughout the day. It works!

Loving By Action

Someone rightly said, "Action speaks louder than words." There is a place for words, but there is also a place for action. Lending a helping hand, being available, all make a lot of difference in relationships. They are ways of saying "I care".

Someone once said that it can be quite frustrating for a woman to be busy doing all the housework, while the man just sits in front of the television enjoying a game of football and from time to time turn around to say to the tired and worn-out woman, "I love you, dear." She knows you love her, at least you have said so. But take a step, help her around the house, it adds credence to your words!

A brother gave this testimony in church:

*"When the Bishop's wife taught us the course **Family Life** at the Bible School, one would have thought she had secretly conducted a research on me, because every aspect of the lecture was directed at me, positively or negatively! After the second day of the course, I got home and saw that my wife had to carry 20 crates of soft drinks down the road, while she was at the same time getting dinner together.*

Unknown to her, I packed all the crates into my car and took them there for her. When I got back home, behold, my wife was at the door, and seeing that I had packed all the crates down the road, she started singing and dancing! Children of God, that was all the service I needed to have rendered in my family; and ever since, it's been tranquility, joy and peace galore!"

Touching

Sometimes, a touch speaks just as much as words. It communicates "I am with you." It keeps the fire burning all the time.

Some families never touch each other. They're cold and the atmosphere in the house is usually tense. But a touching produces warmth. When a husband for instance, puts his arms around his wife, it brings warmth that neither money nor words can produce.

Husband and wife, study to be romantic. Couples are to be "ravished" by each other's love! "*...be thou ravished always with her love*" (Proverbs 5:19). "Ravished" means transported by delight. It will work wonders for your family!

Giving Of Gifts

God so loved the world, He gave His son! If you claim to love, it must find expression in giving. A thoughtful little gift at the right time can work wonders! You must make it a point of duty to remember special days such as birthdays, anniversaries, special occasions, and share the joy of the moment by exchanging gifts. These were the things you did while courting, you shouldn't let them slip by, just because you are now married.

A gift at the right time to your spouse can enhance your relationship and make it more precious. Remember Elkanah and Hannah? Elkanah was sensitive to the needs of his wife. He had so mastered the art of ministering to Hannah's emotional needs that he could say to her, **"...Am not I better to thee than ten sons?"** (I Samuel 1:8)

Husband, there may be times when your wife is down physically. Remember that "love is medicine". At such times, all you need to do is to show a little more love and she will be okay! Some kind words, a little physical touch, some kisses or a little gift from you will do the magic! You could use the time she would have spent at the doctor's office, to demonstrate your love to her and you wouldn't have to spend money on drugs!

I will never forget an experience I had some years back. I was down physically and my husband went out one of those days and came back with a little beautifully wrapped gift, which he personally presented to me, expressing his love to me. Could you believe that that little act of love from him brought me health and I never needed any more medication? Many years have passed, but I still keep that gift, well preserved till today. There is no woman who hates to be loved.

These are little things, which have the ability to lift your marriage. Love is medicine! We love those who are precious and honour them.

How Did Christ Love?

Let's see in practical terms how Jesus loves, and how He expects us to love.

> *Love is very patient and kind, never jealous or envious, never boastful or proud,*
>
> *Never haughty or selfish or rude. Love does not demand its own way. It is not irritable or touchy. It does not hold grudges and will hardly even notice when others do it wrong.*
>
> 1 Corinthians 13:4-5 (TLB)

Patience and Kindness

Jesus, while He walked the earth was an epitome of patience and kindness. He tolerated, accommodated and endured with His disciples and His world. He could have given up out of anger, but He didn't.

Going beyond His disciples to the Jews at large, whose

sick He healed, whose dead He raised and whose demoniacs He freed, Jesus was still the epitome of patience. He closed His eyes to their jeerings and went to the cross for all our sakes.

Kind? Jesus was kindness personified! Many miracles He wrought were based on compassion.

Now, God's Word instructs husbands to love as He did. Many things try our patience as husbands, most of all, imperfect wives. But if Christ was patient with us, then husbands ought to endure with their wives. Jesus often had to repeat a matter over and over and still his disciples didn't catch on. He didn't abuse them or throw them out, rather He was patient with them. With a thief like Judas, a doubter like Thomas or a weakling like Simon, Jesus could still call them friends and joint-heirs with Him of eternal life. That's not fondness, that's love!

If you want to keep from becoming faint-hearted and weary, think about His patience as sinful men did such terrible things to Him.

> *After all, you have never yet struggled against sin and temptation until you sweat great drops of blood.*
> Hebrews 12:3-4 (TLB)

Never Jealous Or Envious

Can you imagine Jesus being jealous of the

achievements of the 70, as they went out in twos and wrought great deliverances? No! Jesus only replied: ...***He that believeth on me, the works that I do shall he do also; and greater works than these shall he do; because I go unto my Father.*** (John 14:12)

Jesus' love compelled Him not to envy the works of His disciples, but to desire that they did greater works. Likewise, husbands need not feel threatened by their wives' successes. Rather, they should wish them well and encourage them to put in their best. Even if the wife earns more money, perfect love places a demand on the husband, to desire only good for her.

Jealous men are insecure. They fear the success of their wives; they hate to see them move ahead in life. But this is not right! Loving as Christ means, being the catalyst for your wife's success, not a deterrent. Whatever I have come to know in God today, the bulk of it was learnt from my dear husband. Were it not for his love and encouragement, I don't know what life would have been like for me.

Never Boastful or Proud

Jesus never spoke proudly of Himself, He never boasted. Everything He said and did pointed to God the Father.

...***The Son can do nothing of himself, but what he***

33

seeth the Father do...

John 5:19

Jesus had cause to brag about His works, humility, kindness, but His eyes were focused on God and on the ones He had come to save. Some husbands tend to get carried away with the things they provide in the house and are misled to think: "I am the breadwinner in this house, I do so and so, I give and give and give!" However, when you realise that you have, only because He (God) provided, your language will change.

This is one great secret I have learnt from my husband. As we both acknowledge God as the doer and not ourselves, but walking in humility, God keeps supplying all our needs. That can become your own testimony too.

Not Selfish, Haughty or Rude

"Me, myself and I", has destroyed so many homes. Another name for it is selfishness. Marriage is built on selflessness and courtesy. Jesus, our perfect example, was not selfish. He relinquished His throne to live on the earth, for $33^1/_2$.

> *For ye know the grace of our Lord Jesus Christ, that, though he was rich, yet for your sakes he became poor, that ye through his poverty might be rich.*
>
> 2 Corinthians 8:9

Jesus could have held on to His glory and refused to die the death of sinners, but He closed His eyes to the humiliation on the cross. Now, He has a name exalted above all other names, and at the mention of which all knees must bow.

Husbands must pay the price of selflessness, if they want an enviable marriage. Rudeness is not love. Men who make a practice of speaking rudely to their wives and vice versa, to prove their headship, are missing it. Derogatory remarks and sarcasm do not please God.

Husbands are commanded to love their wives, and this means being courteous and respectful. As a husband, if you are disrespectful to your wife, your house-helps, relatives and children will follow suit. It is absolutely wrong!

Does Not Demand Its Own Way

Love does not demand its own way! That does not mean that the man should become subservient, no! The key word here is "demand". This word means "to claim as a right." Love means asking, "Could you do this please?" You're not begging, neither are you rude. It's a mixture of authority and courtesy.

Pleasant words are as an honeycomb, sweet to the

soul, and health to the bones.

Proverbs 16:24

Not Irritable Or Touchy

This means not being over sensitive. Some people are offended at the slightest thing. They just flare up and go off the handle. Some are very touchy. Husbands, learn to desensitise your nerves! If Jesus had been oversensitive, He would have fought the Pharisees who always sought to trap him. Your wife is neither a Pharisee nor a Sadducee!

Great peace have they which love thy law: and nothing shall offend them.

Psalm 119:165

Great peace settles in the heart of those who love God's law; nothing offends them. They have every cause to take offence, but by virtue of the Word they have contacted, nothing moves them. Jesus lived a life free of offences. Couples must too, if they want their marriage to work.

Does Not Hold Grudges Or Notice When It's Wronged

A grudge, is an angry feeling against a person, for something he has done in the past; it leads to

THE PILLAR OF LOVE

unforgiveness. Love forgives and forgets. It does not keep record of wrongs. There is nothing as frustrating as knowing that a little book exists, in which all your misdeeds are recorded for future references. God forgives us and forgets our sins; we too need to forgive one another as Christ does (Ephesians 4:32).

A Word Of Caution

Love does not necessarily say "Yes" always. There are times when love must say "No". Husband, times when your wife needs to be corrected must not be overlooked. Learn to say "No" when necessary, without feeling guilty.

There was a time when Jesus turned to Peter and said: ...*Get thee behind me Satan...* (Matthew 16:23). He didn't hate Peter, but Peter needed to be reprimanded then and Jesus did not spare him, else he would have crashed His destiny.

> *All scripture is given by inspiration of God, and is profitable for doctrine, for reproof, for correction, for instruction in righteousness:*
> 2 Timothy 3:16

If you have an ill-behaved wife, you are to be blamed, because you know her more than any other person. You know how in your bedroom she abuses, insults, shouts you down and disobeys your instructions, yet you do nothing about it, all in the name of love. That's not love, it's foolishness. Someday, she will do it in the open and then you will be terribly embarrassed. So, why not do a good job at home! Be the man, that is the divine order.

My husband and I are practical about demonstrating love to one another. There are times when out of love he corrects me on certain issues, including the kind of clothes I wear, relationships to keep, etc. Christ does not leave the Church to do just what she wants, whether good or bad. No! He keeps cleansing us by the washing of water by the Word (Ephesians 5: 26, 27)

Why does He do that? He wants to take away every spot, wrinkle and any such thing.

The relationship between the Church and Christ is synonymous with that of the husband and wife. Therefore, you have the responsibility to keep washing your wife, until every spot and wrinkle is done away with. For example, when you want to iron a wrinkled dress, what do you do? You sprinkle some water on it, allow the iron to be very hot, and then smoothen it out. In the same way, by the Word and firmness, you smoothen out the wrinkles in your wife's life. Remember Adam? He failed to iron out the wrinkle in Eve's life, so she put the entire family in trouble. It is wonderful to know also that God did not blame Eve, but Adam. God will hold you accountable for anything that happens in your home. You have no room for excuses. So, rise up to your responsibility.

3

Learning Submission

Wives, submit yourselves unto your own husbands, as unto the Lord

Ephesians 5:22

In God's divine order, submission from a wife to her husband is a necessary requirement for making marriage work. It is also a command from God (Genesis 3:16). From scripture, we understand that His commandments are not grievous. Although, sometimes, submission may appear as foolishness to the world, but to the believer it is wisdom. By this wisdom, many women have won their husbands to the Lord and several have kept their homes from falling apart.

Submission means willingly putting oneself under the authority of another. In Ephesians 5:21-24, apostle Paul communicates the mind of God concerning submission:

Submitting yourselves one to another in the fear of God.

Wives, submit yourselves unto your own husbands, as unto the Lord.

For the husband is the head of the wife, even as Christ is the head of the church: and he is the saviour of the body.

Therefore as the church is subject unto Christ, so let the wives be to their own husbands in every thing.
Therefore as the church is subject unto Christ, so let the wives be to their own husbands in every thing.

Single ladies, before you agree to marry any man, ensure that you are willingly ready to put yourself under his authority, else that marriage may never work. Married ladies, don't wait for enforced submission. Willingly put yourself under your husband's authority.

There are some key things you must understand about submission from the above scripture.

Submission has four major components: Humility, Obedience, Respect and Love.

Pride hinders so many women from submitting. But pride is destructive, it must not be haboured (1 Peter 5:5). Also, obedience and respect are principal requirements in submission, because a husband you cannot obey and respect, you cannot claim to be submissive to. Finally on that note, remember your husband needs to be loved. Learn to keep showering your love on him (Titus 2:4). That way you make your marriage work.

Your Submission Is First To God

Submitting yourselves **one to another in the fear of God.**

Ephesians 5: 21

The Amplified Bible renders that last bit this way: *"...***Out of reverence for Christ (the Messiah, the Anointed One***)."* As a believer, your heart must first be submitted to Christ, before it can successfully submit to others.

Before a woman can submit to her husband, she must first learn to submit to God. The degree to which she yields herself to the commands of God, determines the degree to which she will yield to her husband. The husband must also submit himself to God, because it is the extent to which he submits to God that will determine the degree to which his wife will submit to him.

Christian women who are submissive to God are those who exalt His Word and are doers of it. Only such women can genuinely submit to their husbands. Before your horizontal relationship can blossom (relationship between you and your husband), your vertical relationship (with God) must first be in place.

Submitting to God has always brought tremendous blessings. For instance, Abraham submitted to the Word of the Lord when he took Isaac up to mount Moriah to sacrifice him. This act of obedience moved God to bless him (Genesis 22:1-17).

Jesus, too, forgot about the pleasures of heaven and yielded to the Father's request. He did not consider His life, but agreed to go to the cross. But with the cross came the crown and from His sweat, sweet came (Philippians. 2:9).

When you are ready and eager to obey God's commandment to submit to your husband, then you are ready to eat the good of marriage (Isaiah 1:19). A lack of understanding of this truth is why marriage is not working for some.

Store up God's Word in your heart and trust that at times when you are expected to submit, God's Holy Spirit will quicken an appropriate verse in you and strengthen you to obey.

Secondly, ask God to create in you a willingness to submit to your spouse. You need to ask in order to receive and He will grant the needed grace.

Submission Is A Command

God commanded the man to love his wife, and the woman to submit to his authority. It is something every wife must do. Failure to embrace submission as a command from God, has brought so much heartache into several homes. God in His omniscience, knows that without this all-important ingredient, no matter how anointed the couple are, that marriage simply cannot work.

Ephesians 5:22 clearly equates obedience to one's own husband, with obedience to the Lord. In fact, it says in the Living Bible translation that the wife should submit to the husband "**in the same way**". That is, with the same reverence with which you would treat God, you are expected to treat your own spouse. This explains why Sarah submitted so much to Abraham and called him "lord." Whosoever wants to keep her soul from destruction, must determine to keep this commandment.

He that keepeth the commandment keepeth his own soul; but he that despiseth his ways shall die.

Proverbs 19:16

When a woman purposes to willingly put herself under the control or authority of her husband, she is obeying God's command and she cannot miss her reward (Proverbs 13:13).

45

Submission Is Of The Heart

Submission flows from the heart. Women who battle with submission, do so because God's Word has not gained entrance into their hearts. You may hear a message on submission and receive it with joy, but you need to let it sink into you heart.

Until submission takes root in your heart, it does not last. You may submit for a little while, but later revert to your former rebellious ways.

Woman, make your heart tender to the Word of God, that you may enjoy the 30, 60, and a 100-fold returns in your family (Luke 8:15). Receive the Word, keep it and work at it with patience, until your fruits begin to show. God watches the heart, so you must keep your heart with all diligence.

The state of your heart determines the words of your mouth; rebellious thoughts lead to rebellious acts. Therefore, submission must be in thought, word and action.

One key you can employ to help your thought life, is to watch what you spend your time reading and listening to, feed your eyes upon and of course, the company you keep.

You must purpose to separate from and sever all links with people and books that teach values contrary to those in the Bible. Woman, think good about your husband. Wish him well in your thoughts, for that is where submission begins!

Submission By Your Words

Submission can be reflected in the words you speak. How do you address your husband? Some women talk to their husbands rudely, using derogatory words. No, it's very wrong! You can convey submission, rebellion, or indifference by your choice of words. By speaking right and gracious words, you will draw your husband closer. Words can be correctly used to bring you favour with your spouse. Without doubt, right words spoken at the right time are of great value (Proverbs 25:11).

A sister said she had always encountered difficulties in her home, because she could not control her tongue. She gave this testimony:

"I had always encountered difficulties in my home because I could not control my tongue. I was so sharp-tongued that anytime my husband wanted to speak or correct me, I would end up quarrelling with him. There was no humility in me and I knew it was the cause of so many problems in our home.

Coming for the 1994 Women Convention, I decided I needed a practical solution. As the woman of God ministered, I desired the same spirit of humility and submission at work in her. I then decided that like the woman with the issue of blood touched Jesus' garment and was made whole, I would touch the woman of God and receive my heart's desire.

After the ministration, I went forward to the altar and embraced Mummy Oyedepo, and she said to me, 'It is well'. That was it! All became well with my life and my tongue received a touch. My husband noticed that a new life had emerged in me."

In Your Actions Too

Be beautiful inside, in your hearts, with the lasting charm of a gentle and quiet spirit which is so precious to God.

That kind of deep beauty was seen in the saintly women of old, who trusted God and fitted into their husbands' plans.

Sarah for instance, obeyed her husband Abraham, honouring him as head of the house. And if you do the same, you will be following in her steps like good daughters and doing what is right; then you will not need to fear (offending your husbands).

1 Peter 3:4-6 (TLB)

Sarah is a good example of a covenant woman and we are told to emulate her life-style of obedience (Isaiah 51:2). Her name is also mentioned in God's hall of faith, because she was an obedient woman (Hebrews 11:11).

Obedience is doing what you are told to do. Make a practice of doing what your husband tells you to do. In so doing, you are reflecting submission in your actions. Some women always advance reasons why what they are asked to do will not work. But that is not submission in practice. Obedience is one cheap way to win your husband's love. Let your action reflect submission.

Submission Must Be Absolute

Therefore as the church is subject unto Christ, so let the wives be to their own husbands in every thing.
Ephesians 5:24

The Word of God is the final authority on everything for the Church. The Church of Jesus is subject in everything to the Word, which is Christ. Whatever God's Word says, we do in obedience. Woman, God's Word says you must submit in everything to your husband. When you do, you make it easy for him to fulfil his covenant responsibilities to you.

Your duty is to ensure that you fulfil your obedience in everything, and if an injustice is done to you, God will be the judge. Whether your husband is an unbeliever or not, as long as he does not tell you to do things that are contrary to scriptures, you are to obey. This includes obedience in spiritual, mental, material or financial matters.

In Spiritual Matters

> *...Who trusted God and fitted in with theirs husbands' plans.*
>
> *1 Peter 3:5 (TLB)*

A woman must first identify with her husband's calling or vision. It is unscriptural for a woman to seek to pursue a vision or a spiritual project, when her husband is against it. In fact, the Bible says you are to "fit in". Like a part of a jigsaw puzzle, you must adapt and adjust to your husband's dreams. As you do so joyfully, if God has given you a different ministry, your husband will gladly back you up. I am a living proof of this.

Out of zeal, a number of women take offence when their husbands don't allow them to take up certain activities in their local churches. By applying wisdom via prayers, a woman can get her husband to change his mind about her kingdom interests. Never should you resort to quarrelling. Remember, prayer changes things.

Another way of winning a man's heart is by a "respectful, pure behaviour" (1 Peter 3:1). Unbelieving husbands, who refuse to pay attention to their wives' witnessing, will respond to their godly lifestyles.

Physically

An understanding that your body belongs to your husband and his to you, will make it easier to yield your body to him. For instance, you may not feel like making love with your husband, but out of submission, you freely do so if he so desires. Your husband will have more respect for you and go out of his way to please you. Whether he does or not, however, knowing you are obeying God's commandment will bring you so much satisfaction. Don't keep your body from your spouse with the aim of punishing him, it's unscriptural.

Physical submission also includes our outward appearance, e.g. cooking, taking care of the home, etc. If your husband doesn't like a particular way you wear your hair, makeup or clothes, please be submissive enough to change it.

You owe it to your husband to dress in a way that is pleasing to him and to cook the type of food he likes, rather than say, "That's not how I learnt to cook!" Also, cater for the home in a way that will make him happy. If as a wife, you seek to please your husband, God will make your life pleasant.

Financially

Two must become one in the area of finances as well.

By opening up to one another in your finances, you help ensure that money will not be exalted as a god. It is the love of money that makes many deal dishonestly with one another in marriage. Some wives go to the extent of hiding money away in banks, without the knowledge of their husbands.

Money is merely a medium of buying and selling, it must not be a channel for the devil to gain access into the family. I don't hide away money from my husband and my openness has motivated him to trust me completely. As husband and wife, whether you keep a joint account or separate accounts, you must ensure that there is openness. This is the only way to avoid shame.

Let me give a word of caution here. Submission must be absolute, that is true. But the Bible gives a condition:

> **Wives, submit yourselves unto your own husbands, as unto the Lord.**
>
> Ephesians 5:22

Submission is as *unto the Lord*. When a man wants his wife to engage in practices contrary to the Word of God, she is scripturally not expected to submit. Submitting on such occasions is absolute foolishness! This must, however, be done in wisdom.

I read about a couple sometime ago. The man was

engaged in bestiality; he slept with animals and involved his wife too. He often made her sleep with dogs, while he watched. The result was that their three children were demon-possessed. The woman should have refused outright! Making heaven is more important. We must not compromise our faith.

In Africa, where some people consult with witch doctors for divination, healing, etc, wives must be exceptionally careful not to be lured into this practice. Idolatry is sin against God, there is no justification for it. In case your husband is not born again, constantly ask God for wisdom on how to submit to him the Bible way, without displeasing God or missing heaven!

Benefits Of Submission

There is a way a man would speak good of his wife, praise and respect her, that would make people wonder if he has been "charmed." That's one of the benefits of submission. It **wins a man's heart!**

As Christ is the head of the man, so is the man head over his wife. If she willingly submits to him, she would have a **covering** spiritually, financially and physically.

Even the natural man knows that once a woman wears the wedding band on her finger, she becomes a "madam", not to be addressed as a girl any longer. No matter her age, she is respected by the society. But once she steps out of the union and becomes an 'Ms.' (neither Mrs. nor Miss), the blessed covering is removed and all types of men come to her, probably ridiculing her.

Secondly, submission always **enthrones** and promotes. Jesus submitted Himself to the plan of redemption, therefore God exalted Him, giving Him a name above all names. If by submission, Jesus our perfect example ascended His throne, by submission you also will be glorified and ascend the throne that God has reserved for you in your home.

Woman, there is a throne for you in your marriage and family, but you need the instrument of submission to ascend it.

Submission also triggers genuine **care**. Once you learn to submit, you have compelled your husband to care for you. It is also an avenue for fostering **unity**.

Submission Is A Seed

When you sow corn seeds, you expect to reap corn. When you sow beans, you expect a harvest of beans. Every natural farmer understands this process. When a woman sows the seed of submission, she stands to reap a bountiful harvest of lifting and honour.

...Before honour is humility.

Proverbs 15:33

But the natural farmer also understands that there's a time lag between planting and harvest time. It is not the day you plant your seedlings that they germinate, grow and yield fruit. The farmer must patiently tend his crop, watering, weeding and nurturing it until there is a bountiful harvest. Believing women who are married to unbelieving men, especially, need to strongly embrace this principle. They must keep nurturing the seed of submission they have sown in their homes, until the man is won to Jesus.

If a woman does not sow seeds of submission to her husband, her children will in turn rebel in every way against her (Genesis 8:22). Woman, do you find your children, co-workers, subordinates and other people generally rebelling against you? It may be because you don't submit to your own husband back at home. Remember that when you sow a seed, you reap it back in many folds.

Pride, is a major reason why some women hate to submit. The natural man is egocentric. But self must be dethroned and Jesus enthroned, if you want the glorious harvest of success in your home. Pride goes before destruction. Humility exalts, better embrace it!

Prayer makes submission cheap. It's called prayer power, and it's been a great asset to me as well as to countless other women. Rather than arguing and quarrelling, go to God in prayer, present your strong reasons, and see things change. Prayer becomes more effective, when light from the Word gains entrance into the heart.

If you desire success in your marriage, use the instrument of submission, it works!

4

The Marriage Bed

When a man and a woman enter into the covenant of marriage, they enter into a formal agreement which is legally binding.

Every legal contract has a seal, including marriage. The seal is in the consummation of the marriage — sexual intercourse. Sex is sacred to God, because He is a God of covenants. For every covenant God makes, He gives a seal of the covenant (Genesis 9:12-13; 17:9-11; Romans 6:4; Acts 8:36). So then, we begin to understand why God's Word emphatically states:

Marriage is honourable in all, and the bed undefiled: but whoremongers and adulterers God will judge.
                                                            Hebrews 13:4

The bed must remain undefiled, because sex is the seal of the marriage covenant. Any sexual relationship engaged in outside marriage, breaks the seal and attracts a punishment. Therefore, you must never get involved in it. However, if you have already defiled the bed, repent and ask God for forgiveness, then forsake it immediately.

God created the world first, then gave man a body with which to function effectively in the physical, material world.

He then commanded man:

> *...Be fruitful, and multiply, and replenish the earth...*
>
> Genesis 1:28

He gave the man and the woman reproductive organs with which to carry out this command. There is therefore, nothing dirty or unclean about sexual intercourse for the married.

It is true that as a result of the fall, man perverted the beautiful act of love making. What was designed to give man utmost pleasure, a sense of satisfaction and dignity, became the avenue through which man expressed carnality. Like the wild beasts, man cheapened the sexual union. He defiled what God had intended as a seal for the covenant of marriage (Romans 1:24-29).

Marriage is only honourable when the bed is undefiled. If sex is engaged in before marriage, the honour that a marriage enjoys from God and men is removed. Even the value each spouse places on the other will be affected.

Marital love or sex within the context of marriage is a

celebration of the covenant of marriage! God's creation of sexual union was for good and not for bad. However, any good thing can be perverted when wrongly used.

Sexual Union Is Of God

Let's look in details at God's purpose for sexual intercourse within the marriage institution.

For Procreation

God chose this unique method to replenish the earth. He designed the sexual act as the medium for procreation.

And Adam knew *Eve his wife; and she conceived, and bare Cain...*

Genesis 4:1

Paraphrased, the above scripture would read—"**And Adam had marital sex with his wife and she conceived...**" This along with other scriptures prove that God designed marital sex for procreation.

For Pleasure

Let thy fountain be blessed: and rejoice with the wife of thy youth. Let her be as the loving hind and pleasant roe; let her breasts satisfy thee at all times; and be thou ravished always with her love.

Proverbs 5:18,19

God intended that aside from the purpose of procreation, marital sex should give pleasure. I saw a write-up that should help you to understand better what we are talking about. It says:

"Over the centuries, the extremists justified this *coming together* to be just for one purpose only — to *multiply*. Anything else was considered worldly... A woman was considered simply a child-bearing machine. Those who believed sex had an additional purpose — to refurbish, to motivate, to revitalise — were tagged as dangerous. Religious leaders taught that such thinking would be an open invitation to all the devices of Satan.

Marital sex or sex in marriage was designed to give one of the highest forms of sensual pleasure ever created. Paul described it as a benevolence, which means a gift that blesses."[1]

> **Let the husband render unto the wife due benevolence: and likewise also the wife unto the husband.**
>
> I Corinthians 7:3

Having a wholesome approach to marital sex, will heal many wounds in homes. Statistics show that families where the husband and wife enjoy each other sexually, are the happiest homes. For the breasts of a man's wife to satisfy him means for the two of them to have pleasure in marital sex.

For Intimacy

> ... *Abimelech king of the Philistines looked out at a window, and saw, and, behold, Isaac was sporting with Rebekah his wife.*
>
> Genesis 26:8

"Sporting", as has been suggested by Bible scholars, may not be marital sex or actual sexual relationship, but foreplay. It must have been intimate enough to suggest to Abimelech that Rebecca was Isaac's wife. This, too, is a good and perfect gift from a good and perfect God. "Playing" intimately with your spouse is not wrong, but rather brings you closer.

That's why several times, the Bible uses the word "know" to describe the intimate, physical relationship between husband and wife. One of God's intentions for marriage is for the couple to really know one another until they become truly one.

> ...*For this cause shall a man leave father and mother, and shall cleave to his wife: and they twain shall be one flesh?*
>
> *Wherefore they are no more twain, but one flesh...*
>
> Matthew 19:5-6

The joining to one's spouse also describes the act of sex. For as a man is joined in physical union to his wife, they become one in a way not possible with any other person. It is, however, only within the context of marriage that guilt does not accompany sex. If both man and woman work at making the act of sex more than just an avenue for procreation or the releasing of tension, it becomes a means of enhancing intimacy.

In itself, the act of sex is a fellowship —giving and receiving tender love. I believe that it brought comfort to Isaac after the death of his mother, Sarah; because it provided a means of intimate fellowship with someone he loved (Genesis 24:67).

To avoid fornication

One other reason God designed the marriage bed was to ensure that man has a legitimate avenue for releasing sexual tension. Outside the sanctity of marriage, any sexual act, from petting to sporting, etc, is sin.

> *...It is good for a man not to touch a woman. Nevertheless, to avoid fornication, let every man have his own wife, and let every woman have her own husband.*
>
> I Corinthians 7:1-2

The Act Of Marriage

Have you ever wondered what the scene was like, the first night Adam "knew" his wife Eve? Eden means delight or pleasure. Now, imagine a garden created in Eden. It must have been beautiful, picturesque, to say the least! Not polluted by sin or vulgar imaginations. God must have been pleased to see that the man and his wife were comfortable in their "home."

Right from that time, the act of marriage holds its greatest appeal in an edenic environment. The world tries to imitate this by creating "get-aways" for newly weds, particularly in the west where newly wedded couples are expected to go on honeymoon. But the idea was borrowed from the Church. That is why every intimate session with your partner should be memorable. The room must be neat and bedsheets fresh and attractive.

Both partners should realise that smelly armpits and bad breath can put one off! If we genuinely care for each other, then taking the pains to clean up is essential. That is how the Delilahs of the world keep the Samsons trapped. They know how to make sex appealing.

Christian women in particular need to be delivered from making the act of sex boring and unexciting. Most take advantage of the fact that their spouses cannot go elsewhere, to be a big put-off to them.

The beloved of Solomon took her time to make herself a delight (Songs of Solomon 4:9-16). It is not surprising that the man yearned to come into his beloved's garden and eat pleasant fruits. She prepared herself and her environs for him.

Sometimes, a wife must bend to the demands of her husband. It is not always that she wants sex when he does, but as she purposes to bring a smile to her husband's face, the Holy Spirit enables her to flow along with him. But to constantly come up with excuses, putting the man off, is to defraud him. Don't do it! As husband and wife, know that your bodies now belong to one another.

> *The wife hath not power of her own body, but the husband: and likewise also the husband hath not power of his own body, but the wife. Defraud ye not one the other...*
>
> I Corinthians 7:4-5

Someone once said that probably more fraud is practised in marriage than in any other area of life. This is very true. "Not now! I have a headache." "Why don't you think about something else for a change?" "I am too tired", or "I am too busy." The writer crowned it all by declaring, "Marital fraud is an offence...and dullness is a sin."2 We all know that there is no glory for those practising fraud. That is why some homes lack glory and beauty.

There is a secret in this. If the husband gives his wife

the love and attention she desires and she "submits" her body to him, they will find that the sacrifices they may need to make in the process is worth it. They will both discover that while sex is not everything, it is the engine oil that keeps the marriage car running smoothly. To be successful in this area, is to successfully block any loopholes that might give the enemy a foothold in one's marriage. When husband and wife are satisfied sexually, their level of productivity in other areas will be maximum!

Things That Defile The Marriage Bed

Marriage is honourable in all, and the bed undefiled...
Hebrews 13:4

Marriage was designed to deposit unique honour on man. Yet, from Hebrews 13:4, we see that God attaches a condition for honour— the bed must be undefiled!

For The Singles

The marriage bed, as its name implies, is for the married only. To engage in sexual intercourse as a single, is a sin against your own conscience and against God.

As was earlier mentioned, it is only within the context of marriage that guilt does not accompany sex. Defiling the marriage bed as a single, is the quickest route to shame in marriage, whether you are marrying the person involved or not. I receive letters from singles, who are troubled by guilt, shame and other woes, because they couldn't control themselves and engaged in sex before marriage.

If you are still single, steer clear of sex till you are married. Don't be pushed into it because of anxiety. Be patient and you will find out that it is worth waiting.

A 40-year-old single lady attended our Women Convention in 1994. She had been anxious and disturbed about not being married yet. However, on getting to the convention, she decided to exercise her faith. As the ministration was going on, she caught the prophetic words that came forth concerning her situation. Before the end of that year, she met her husband and they got married. The following year, they were blessed with a baby! It pays to wait on God.

> *Flee fornication. Every sin that a man doeth is without the body; but he that committeth fornication sinneth against his own body.*
>
> *...Your body is the temple of the Holy Ghost...ye are not your own.*
>
> I Corinthians 6:18-19

Until you are legally married and joined in the church,

you are not permitted to engage in sexual intercourse.

The Bible enjoins singles to present their bodies as a living sacrifice unto the Lord (Romans 12:1). In the dispensation of the law, sacrificial animals were robust, good looking (without bodily scars), and without blemish, or else, they were unacceptable before God. In like manner, God commands you to separate yourself from sexual sins as well as caressing and the like, as these defile your body.

> *...It is good for a man not to touch a woman.*
> *I Corinthians 7:1*

We live in modern times, where a lot of the virtues our parents upheld are pushed aside, as being old fashioned. No more are those engaged to be married chaperoned. There is a lot more liberality among the new generation. Thank God the Bible was not inspired by man's customs and ideologies. What is contained therein was inspired by the Holy Spirit, Who is eternal, and He says, **"It is not good for a man to touch a woman"**.

God's Word cannot become obsolete, His Word cannot become old fashioned. Chastity is as important today as it was in the Bible days. Simply because the world does not see its importance, does not change anything. Before God, it's just as essential a foundation for a good marriage, as it was when the Bible was written.

Marriage is a covenant, and sex the seal of the covenant. As earlier said, the breaking of the hymen by one's husband is crucial and has a lot of spiritual significance.

Covenants are sealed by the shedding of blood, so that they cannot easily be broken. On the wedding night, as the marriage is consummated, God expects to see the hymen break and blood flow, to seal the covenant of marriage between husband and wife.

Each time you engage in sex, a part of you is given to the other party. A man of God put it this way: "If you break two eggs in a bowl, when they mix, you will never be able to perfectly separate them again."

Because marriage is for life, you will be secure, in that you are not giving yourself to someone that will take a part of you and run away with it. Chastity must be taken seriously, no human custom or modern day ideology can change that.

> *But if...the tokens of virginity be not found for the damsel:*
>
> *Then they shall bring out the damsel to the door of her father's house, and the men of the city shall stone her with stones that she die...*
>
> Deuteronomy 22:20-21

The death and resurrection of Jesus have erased this harsh consequence, but we know that the deed remains as a scar on your conscience. God's honour is reserved for the pure. However, if you are single but no longer a virgin, probably you lost your virginity before you got born again, remember:

> *...The times of this ignorance God winked at; but now commandeth all men every where to repent*
>
> Acts 17:30

> *For if our heart condemn us, God is greater than our heart, and knoweth all things.*
>
> 1 John 3:20

All you need to do is to ask God for forgiveness and then forgive yourself. Refuse to continue living in condemnation.

For The Married

After the solemnisation of a marriage, the rules of abstaining from sex ends. Sex is no longer forbidden; if anything, it becomes an essential part of the union. However, the marriage bed can still be defiled by the married.

> *Marriage is honourable in all, and the bed undefiled: but whoremongers and adulterers God will judge.*
>
> Hebrews 13:4

To defile means to make dirty or unclean. One thing

that definitely pollutes the act of marriage is adultery. The Bible defines it as lying with another man's wife (Leviticus 20:10).

If either the man or the woman is married and has sexual intercourse with anyone other than his or her spouse, he has committed adultery and has opened up for God's judgment.

Secondly, marriage is founded upon a very delicate material called trust. One cannot afford to be caught in the webs of adultery, because when trust is broken, suspicion sets in , which might eventually break up the marriage. Another thing adultery does is that the respect your spouse had for you is shattered. By committing adultery therefore, you literally take the honour God bestows upon you and cast it before swine. The Bible says:

> *Give not that which is holy unto the dogs, neither cast ye your pearls before swine, lest they trample them under their feet, and turn again and rend you.*
>
> Matthew 7:6

When your honour is trampled upon, nothing remains of it.

When you are married, there is a hedge of protection round about you, which is broken when you commit adultery, and anything negative can happen as a result.

Ecclesiastes 10:8 says: ***Whoso breaketh an hedge, a serpent shall bite him***.

The serpents of life are biting hard on many marriages and families today, because the hedge is broken by unfaithfulness. They lack honour and fulfilment because they have polluted the marriage bed. Please be warned, God is not playing with words. If you commit adultery, the serpents will strike at your home.

Let's examine a dimension of adultery often overlooked. Take for instance, a beautiful woman walks by, a married man looks at her from the crown of her head to the sole of her feet, he admires her. She passes by, but her figure remains heavily imprinted upon his mind. God's Word says even looking lustfully at a woman is the same as committing adultery with her.

> ***...Whosoever looketh on a woman to lust after her hath committed adultery with her already in his heart.***
>
> Matthew 5:28

David was a man after God's own heart. He loved God and walked uprightly before the Lord. Nevertheless, a day came when he sent his lieutenants to war, but tarried in Jerusalem. At evening time, king David strolled out upon the roof top. His heart must have been on the battlefield. He must have wondered how his men fared.

As he pondered on these, his eyes caught sight of a beautiful woman bathing. One thing led to another, until he slept with the woman, killed her husband and brought destruction upon his family. James 1:14-15 summarises the narrative in 2 Samuel 11 thus:

> *...Every man is tempted, when he is drawn away of his own lust, and enticed.*
>
> *Then when lust has conceived, it bringeth forth sin: and sin, when it is finished, bringeth forth death. Then when lust has conceived, it bringeth forth sin: and sin, when it is finished, bringeth forth death.*

The first place David committed adultery with Bathsheba was in his heart. Don't let vain imaginations destroy you, cast them down (2 Corinthians 10:5). Bring every thought to the obedience of the Word.

As married people, there are certain stimuli we can do without. The world relies on pornography to stimulate their sexual appetite. We don't need to do this, because the impressions they leave on the mind have devastating effects.

As a married or single man or woman, each time you see someone of the opposite sex and you lose balance, you cannot control yourself anymore, you sweat from head to toe or begin to stammer; you don't need anyone to tell you that something is wrong somewhere. The earlier you deal with it, by pleading the Blood of Jesus, casting out wrong thoughts and looking away, the better! You can deal with that temptation; it is not above you (1 Corinthians 10:13).

How Far Should We Go?

Many Christian couples ask this question. They wonder what is an acceptable boundary within the sexual union. It is not wrong to ask, because the world has so perverted the act of sex, introducing all manner of techniques into the act of marriage' in a bid to satisfy their sexual drive.

All believers have a measure of the Holy Spirit. You can simply ask Him to lead you aright. God has placed a conscience that is sensitive to His leading in us. Thus we can discern what is an acceptable boundary.

> *But the anointing which ye have received of him abideth in you, and ye need not that any man teach you: but as the same anointing teacheth you of all things, and is truth, and is no lie, and even as it hath taught you, ye shall abide in him.*
>
> I John 2:27

> *All things are lawful unto me, but all things are not expedient...*
>
> I Corinthians 6:12

Nevertheless, fear of crossing the acceptable boundary should not keep you from enjoying the act of sex. It was designed to give pleasure, so make it a return to Eden.

Myths About Marital Sex

So many myths exist about sexual intercourse, even within the context of marriage, especially during the Victorian age, when women were not expected to enjoy it. If a woman did, she was termed "loose". In fact, any woman who showed too much enthusiasm and eagerness was suspected by her husband.

In some African societies too, female babies are circumcised to prevent them from developing strong sexual drives.

Letha Scanzoni described what Church fathers propagated about sexual relationships within marriage: "Peter Lombard and Gratien warned Christians that the Holy Spirit left the room when a married couple engaged in sexual intercourse, even if it were for the purpose of conceiving a child! Other church leaders insinuated that God required sexual abstinence during all holy days and seasons.

"And in addition, couples were advised not to have sexual relationship on Thursdays, in honour of Christ's arrest, on Fridays in memory of His crucifixion, on

Saturdays in honour of the virgin Mary, on Sundays in remembrance of Christ's resurrection, and on Mondays out of respect for the departed souls (leaving only Tuesday and Wednesday)!" How amusing!

God created sex to give man pleasure. However, *...Wisdom is profitable to direct*.

5

Understanding Male/Female Differences

As male and female partners in marriage, we must understand and appreciate the peculiarities, which make up our personalities. Men are men and women, women. Understanding the uniqueness of the male gender will help the woman appreciate why her man acts the way he does, thus eliminating problems from the family.

Through wisdom is an house builded; and by understanding it is established.

Proverbs 24:3

God designed the man to be the head of the union. He is the aggressor, the provider. He was designed to take the lead, while the woman is the follower. When anyone tries to change this order, problems arise.

This accounts for why the male sexual drive is generally more than that of the woman. Sex is as important as eating, drinking or sleeping to a man, because it provides an avenue for the release of tension. For instance, when faced with important decisions and the like, some men feel the basic way to release tension is through marital relations.

An example of this truth is seen in the life of David and Bathsheba. God declared that the child which was a product of his infidelity would die. David was grieved, and entreated the Lord in sack cloth and ashes for seven days, but the child still died. The moment David learnt of it, he bathed, ate, drank. But 2 Samuel 12:24 records that he:

> ...*Comforted Bathsheba his wife, and went in unto her, and lay with her: and she bare a son, and he called his name Solomon: and the Lord loved him....Comforted Bathsheba his wife, and went in unto her, and lay with her: and she bare a son, and he called his name Solomon: and the Lord loved him.*

What a time to make love! But this is characteristic of the male gender. Bathsheba was a considerate woman, to accept David's love and give in to him.

The woman on the other hand, having worked all day, having attended to the children and done household chores, may find out that at the end of the day, making love is the last thing on her mind: she is simply tired! By nature, she is only ready for the act of marriage when she's rested and relaxed.

She may not desire it as often as does the man, and may be puzzled why the man should. But the two are designed differently. The unique personalities of a husband and wife should contribute to a successful marriage, not destroy it.

Women enjoy conversation, they want to be sure that love making is not just an act, but a time of *intimacy* and *fellowship*. No woman wants to feel used.

Why is it necessary to know all this? Because many are suffering in silence! They have a great marriage generally speaking, but because of a lack of understanding, the marriage bed remains their only source of concern. As it were, it is the only "But" in their marriage and a big one at that! With the help of the Holy Spirit, you can understand the differences in the make-up of your spouse, and with that understanding comes a more fulfilling time.

Husband and wife are meant to be friends, lovers and companions; but only an understanding of the male-female differences will make this possible.

Husband Get To Know Your Wife!

Likewise, ye husbands, dwell with them according to knowledge, giving honour unto the wife, as unto the weaker vessel, and as being heirs together of the grace of life; that your prayers be not hindered.

1 Peter 3:7

Every man should be knowledgeable about his wife. Husband, know your wife's taste for things like toiletries, wears, colours, etc. Know her likes and dislikes. Wife, be knowledgeable about your husband's taste for things like food, colours, etc.

Men and women have the same basic need for self-worth and belonging. However, they usually satisfy these needs differently.

A man derives his sense of self-worth primarily from the respect, recognition and reputation he gets on his job or through professional accomplishments. He draws emotional satisfaction from achieving success in business, becoming financially independent, developing a highly valuable skill or craft, supervising others, becoming "boss", or being appreciated by his fellow workers.

A woman receives her self-esteem at home, by being told that she is appreciated when she prepares a good dinner, dresses beautifully or keeps the house clean and the household in good order. To be complete and contented, the woman must receive praise from four sources: her husband, her children, her work and the Lord Jesus Christ.

So, the man craves for respect from his wife first and then others, while the woman's self-worth is in place when she is loved and appreciated, first by her husband, and then others.

Knowledge without application is a waste. What profit then has knowledge if one cannot apply it to gain freedom? Do you have knowledge? Great! But you must also know how to use it to make your marriage successful.

6

Communicate!

Communication is very vital in marriage. You may not enjoy your marriage, if you and your spouse don't know how to communicate effectively. It is like having gold in a garden, but not knowing how to dig it out. The gold is there, but as long as it is not dug out, you cannot be enriched by it.

The basis of any fruitful and lasting relationship is effective communication. God our Father and our ultimate example proved this to us, by communicating His plans and intentions to those whom He trusted. He spoke clearly to Moses, Samuel, David, right through to Jesus and beyond Him, to those of us who love and serve Him.

Marriage without effective communication never works. A wise man once said, "If you talk together, you stay together" — and it is true.

In times past, particularly in African societies, women

were regarded as mere objects and a part of a man's possessions, and were not consulted on major issues, neither were their views regarded as important. In those days, women stayed married because they had no choice. But that has never been God's arrangement. He made marriage as an avenue for both husband and wife to find fulfilment, and fulfilment comes when there is effective communication.

What Is Communication?

Communication has been defined as the art of passing across news, information, feeling or whatever, to somebody else. Communication is done mostly in words. That is verbal communication. But there is also non-verbal communication, which includes facial expression, etc.

From this definition, one word stands out — **"across"**. Communication is the art of passing across something. Until you successfully pass a message or a thought across to someone else, you cannot be said to have communicated effectively.

Have you ever been to a seminar, where a celebrated professor was guest lecturer and everything he said was well over your head? He may have spoken for hours and all his points salient and grammatically sound; but if no one understood what he said, he cannot be said to have communicated. Communication therefore, is a two-way process, involving talking and listening. Communication is also at two levels, horizontal and vertical. On the horizontal level, it is between man and man, in this case husband and wife; on the vertical it is between God and man. Effective communication with God, makes communication with man productive.

Communication in marriage involves more than passing across a feeling, thought, message or desire. It also involves how a thing is said and when it is said.

In marriage, the long word "communication" is broken down to "communion", which means "sharing of thoughts and feelings." Breaking the word "communion" further, the word "commune" evolves. To commune means to "speak together as close friends."

Communication is a major component that makes oneness possible. The better we communicate, the closer we become. Talking and listening are both vital in communication.

Every time there is a breakdown in communication, what follows is not always pleasant. My husband once said that poor communication is the reason behind brutality in many Christian marriages, today. A lot of things are done on assumption so, frustrations are inevitable. There must be effective communication between family members as a whole, for frustration to be avoided.

Look at Adam and Eve, they were the perfect couple in a perfect home; but they missed it at the point of communication. Adam was presumptuous. He assumed that Eve understood the instructions of the Lord. The devil sensing that there was a break in communication slipped in and beguiled Eve (Genesis 3:1-2).

Men who are too busy to spend quality time with their families are courting trouble. When God gives either the man or his wife a vision or an assignment, they must share it with the other person, explaining gently until it is clearly understood and received. Where the task is not fully understood, the chances of successfully carrying everyone along is slim.

For instance, my children and I fully understand my husband's vision; so it's easy for us to make the necessary sacrifices to ensure he doesn't fail. If I had no deep understanding of my place in his assignment, perhaps there would have been clashes. But we've never quarrelled and this is one of the reasons.

Engaged couples must learn the art of communication too. They must be open and sincere, disclosing issues that may affect the relationship in future. Couples who are in deep waters in their marriage relationships today, are those who walked in dishonesty, those who were so carried away by the outward, that little time was given to talking openly and honestly.

A sister met me some time ago, bemoaning her lot. She said she and her spouse were contemplating divorce. They lived like cat and dog. Probing further, I discovered that the problem did not start after their marriage, but before, while they were still courting. They never spent time talking and getting to know each other. That was why a marriage of just three months was cracking already!

Communicating with your children is important too. You must create time to talk with and listen to them, sharing matters of importance. If you neglect to do this, out of a lack of understanding of your assignments, they may begin to pull down what God is building up. As young as our children are, they know that both my husband and I are sold out to the Kingdom of God. That's why it's easy for my husband and I to obey God. They understand what we are doing.

As busy as my husband is, he still finds time to talk with the children, answering their questions and clarifying all doubts. Why does he do this? In order not to give the devil a foothold in our family! So, open up the communication lines today, it will save you from heartaches tomorrow!

Components Of Communication

There are certain things that make for effective communication in marriage.

Trust

Communication in marriage is not once and for all time; that is, you cannot say, "I opened up once, I don't want to again." There is a need to always keep the communication lines open. This is why trust is the number one component in communication.

You cannot effectively disclose your innermost dreams, desires and thoughts to someone you don't trust. When you trust someone, it means you have full confidence, faith and assurance in that person, that what you have told her will remain confidential. Trust is precious. The one in whom you put your trust must be reliable.

Women complain that while they love to tell their husbands what their fears, hopes and aspirations are, the men say nothing. This may be why from statistics and interviewing a few men, H. Norman Wright concludes: "A major concern for men about intimacy with women is trust...When can they be trusted? What can they be trusted with? Many men believe women perceive information differently, and they share in public what men see as only personal. However, trust is essential, if we are going to be able to communicate always with our spouses.

"What women need to do is learn to be dependable. Most men also fear this type of communication because often times, when there is a disagreement, the wife brings up what he told her in confidence. Once this happens the man withdraws and refuses to open up again."4

Openness and transparency here, are not talking about saying everything and anything that comes to your mind; that may be dumping garbage on your spouse. No! Communication simply entails maintaining an attitude of openness, with nothing to hide.

> *And they were both naked, the man and his wife,*
> *and were not ashamed.*
>
> Genesis 2:25

The man and his wife must work at being trustworthy, for it is only then that they can earn the trust of each other, giving communication a solid foundation. There is no solid foundation for communication outside trust.

Understanding

> *Through wisdom is an house builded; and by*

understanding it is established:

Proverbs 24:3

Homes are established upon understanding. It is the basis for effective communication.

Understanding enables you to read between the lines; it reads eye movements and voice tones and helps soften the harshness of anger.

When your spouse speaks, his words may be few, but because you understand him very well, he successfully communicates. Abigail is described as a woman with a good understanding. She understood the thirst for vengeance in David, as he came against her ill-mannered husband and effectively communicated with him (1 Samuel 25:23-25).

When you understand your husband or wife, less friction is bound to occur. With a good understanding of her man, a woman can pass across things she has observed that he does, which may not be profitable.

Many homes have been destroyed because of misunderstanding. The husband misunderstands his wife's actions, the woman also reads meanings into simple statements made by the man. But the Word says:

Good Understanding givethfavour...

Proverbs 13:15

Openness

...Hide not thyself from thine own flesh.

Isaiah 58:7

When a man takes a woman as wife, the Bible declares that in God's eyes, they are one flesh. In Ephesians 5:28, God declares:

...He that loveth his wife loveth himself....He that loveth his wife loveth himself.

There's a unique fusion that occurs, a merging of two separate individuals into one.

No one keeps secrets from himself. It is not possible for the toe to hurt without the brain knowing it; they are both members of one body. Similarly, God expects that when two become one in holy wedlock, nothing should be kept as secret between them. Both must be open to one another and walk in sincerity.

The devil often leads people into thinking that if they open up completely, they may never be accepted for who they are or that when their spouses hear the whole truth about an issue, they won't love them anymore. But this is a lie. If in the beginning, the man and his wife were naked but did not experience shame, then it follows that if you apply the same principle of openness to your marriage, shame will not be your portion.

When a wound is covered, it tends to fester and worsen; but when it is opened, however, healing comes. Whatever is covered will eventually be exposed. When it comes to light, it may come with shame and disaster (Proverbs 28:13).

Even after marriage, important things that happen in our day-to-day lives should be shared. Openness breeds trust, and trust is the foundation for effective communication. Don't speak in parables. Be truthful in your communication.

For instance, be free to tell your spouse when you're not happy about his/her lack of personal hygiene or anything else. You'll be surprised that it's such little things that cause big problems. Let your conversation be filled with sincerity. Don't tell half truths. A half truth is a whole lie. Good marriages are founded upon effective communication. Learn to discuss freely with your spouse.

Openness is not only for women; men also need to learn the art of opening up to their wives.

The Vehicle For Effective Communication

When a man has goods to transport, he looks for a medium of transportation. He considers the size of the goods and looks for an appropriate vehicle that can carry them. Communication is like the "goods"; it searches also for an appropriate vehicle.

What is the vehicle for effective communication? Words, right words! Two people can say the same thing, but in different ways. One may successfully pass across his message, while the other may not.

Choosing the right words is a must for the man and wife. It is an art that must be learnt. Submerged in one's choice of words is love, respect and submission. The man chooses words that convey his message, without disrespecting his wife or trampling upon her feelings. The woman responds to the seed of right words, by speaking words that boost the ego of her man.

> *Let no corrupt communication proceed out of your mouth, but that which is good to the use of edifying, that it may minister grace unto the hearers.*
>
> Ephesians 4:29

I perceive that this scripture proceeds right from the heart of God for couples. Corrupt communication is the opposite of edifying communication. You can pass across the negative, just as effectively as you can the positive. Any communication that tears down, rips apart or pollutes the mind is corrupt.

Corrupt communication proceeds from the mouth, true. But it has its root in the heart. When all you think about your spouse is negative and your focus is only on his or her deficiencies, eventually all that will proceed out of your mouth will be corrupt. For, *...out of the abundance of the heart the mouth speaks* (Matthew 12:34).

Aim at ministering grace through your words.

If your partner is an introvert, know that he can be coerced into opening up, when you learn how to listen without interruption. You can also ask appropriate questions to encourage him to keep talking. His opinion on various issues can be sought and his suggestions carried out. A wise man once said that words are the most powerful things on earth.

Benefits Of Effective Communication

Intimacy

Someone said, "Men love the benefits of intimacy, but often they are not committed to the work intimacy entails."

One major benefit of effective communication is intimacy. When it is not there, there is no togetherness, no intimacy; so a gap is created and the enemy is given the opportunity to come in. Therefore, effective communication is arrived at, as you learn to effectively share your innermost dreams and aspirations together as man and wife. Communication cements the relationship of a couple. It is mortar that holds a family together.

Self - Awareness And Acceptance

As you open up to one another as man and wife, you learn more about yourselves. With this awareness comes acceptance. You truly learn to love and appreciate one another. Therefore, both parties must be free to ask each other sincere questions, particularly when something is not understood.

For instance, if you notice any negative behaviour in your partner, call his attention to it. As you speak out, you may be surprised how much a blessing such openness can be.

Enhancing Communication

Learning to Listen

Listening is crucial to effective communication, since it involves talking and listening (Proverbs 18:13). A wise man once said, "Good listeners are good lovers".

Some women, who are more talkative than their husbands, fall short in this area, because they talk so much, not giving room to the man to say anything. Men, usually the quieter party, may really not say anything and yet not listen. How? They may just switch off to thinking about what matters most to them.

Communication goes beyond hearing, to being attentive. It's paying close attention to what another is saying. This enables one to be able to make sound decisions and pass good judgement on various issues.

Truthfulness

Truthfulness is an attribute of God. God detests lies and exaggeration. Even when telling the truth is not convenient, you can receive grace to say things exacting as they are, so that you don't create any loopholes for the devil. You must be very truthful in communicating with your family members. My husband says often, "When Christianity lacks character, there is nothing more to it."

Correct Timing

Words are like eggs. They are fragile and delicate. Once broken, they can't be gathered back again. Thus, you must know your spouse so well that you know when to say what and how. Even when you are so overwhelmed by a matter, you can compose yourself to wait for an appropriate time to speak. There is a due season for every spoken word.

... A word spoken in due season, how good is it!
                                                    Proverbs 15:23

Important issues should be wisely but thoroughly discussed. This implies that there is a need to speak, when there is enough time to dig deep into matters. So, wait until there is enough time before raising certain issues.

Pleasing Each Other

The essence of effective communication is to enhance intimacy, unity and love. The words you speak are to edify your spouse and should be aimed at making the relationship better, not to hurt your partner. Please be willing to admit when you are wrong. Don't be too proud to say so.

Motive is the focus here. You may need to ask yourself some pointed questions, before engaging in heartfelt discussions, especially when crucial issues are to be ironed out. Such questions as: Why am I saying this? Will it make us a better couple? What is my motive? Will it destroy our intimacy or make my spouse lose respect for me?

Engaged couples who often ask how far to go when talking about their past, should keep in mind that whatever they know will cause regrets if and when discovered later, must be discussed now. In Christ we are new creatures; the past is past, but certain things which belong to the past affect the present, especially in relationships. So, give the devil no place. If that person is for you, he or she will accept and appreciate you for your sincerity.

The most effective communication in your marriage, will take place after you have spent time in prayer, praise and worship to God. Esther is a good example. She knew that failing to find favour before the king would mean shame and death, so she spent some time in prayers first before approaching him, and her request was granted.

7

Walking In
Wisdom

Marriage can be likened to a house, and every house is built by men, using certain building materials. Wisdom is a good quality material for building your marriage and home.

> *Through wisdom is an house builded; and by understanding it is established:*
>
> Proverbs 24:3

What is wisdom? Wisdom is knowing which way to go. It is knowing how to handle situations and make them produce your desired results. Wisdom is knowing how to make it in life. When you know how to make things work in your family, you are walking in wisdom.

Your marriage can be steady and strong, it can be an example for others to follow. Like Billy Graham, Kenneth Hagin and a host of others, you can have cause to look back and smile during your sixtieth wedding anniversary. But the foundation of your family must be laid in wisdom.

Solomon wanted to establish the kingdom God gave him. So, when God appeared unto him and told him to ask for whatever he wanted, he asked for wisdom to rule God's people, and God gave it to him (I Kings 3:9,12).

You cannot blame God or anyone else for what your home looks like. If it is not the haven you thought it would be, then you have a responsibility to search for a solution. God's Word clearly says:

For every house is builded by some man...

Hebrews 3:4

Wisdom is also the correct application of knowledge. So, before you can walk in wisdom, you must locate the knowledge of the Word and apply it.

God has made provisions for marriage to produce good for you and I, but we have a responsibility to develop that plan. It is like the negative film of a picture. The photographer must spend time in the darkroom developing the negative and come out with a beautiful picture. A negative must be developed, before it becomes enviable.

Stop shifting blame. Accept that you are the builder of

your marriage. God has provided the wisdom to build with. Be diligent and get down to work! There is no prize for the slothful (Ecclesiastes 10:18).

Building a house is not as simple as ABC. It takes planning!

> *For which one of you, intending to build a tower, sitteth not down first, and counteth the cost, whether he have sufficient to finish it?*
>
> *Lest haply, after he hath laid the foundation, and is not able to finish it, all that behold it begin to mock him,*
>
> *Saying, This man began to build, and was not able to finish.*
>
> Luke 14:28-30

Intending couples must sit down during courtship, and contact revelations for outstanding success in family life. From the pattern of God's Word, you can draw up a blueprint for your home. It is not enough to wish, for nothing is built upon wishes. With the Word of God, you can develop godly, workable goals.

Many, whether single or married, are wishing and hoping that their homes will be beautiful, but only time will tell whether or not they have laid a solid foundation. Don't take chances, understand God's provision for a fulfilled family life, and purpose to walk by it.

Build A Godly Expectation

Houses are of different sizes and shapes. The taller, more beautiful houses require more preparation, a deeper foundation, and they cost more. You must first desire a tower, before you can plan to build one. Don't enter marriage without an expectation. If you expect the best, it will be yours (Proverbs 23:18).

Someone once came to me for counselling, and had been having a very tough time in marriage. As she spoke, I discovered that the root cause of her problems was her wrong idea about marriage. She had expected grief and calamity, so when the storms rose against her marriage, she began to say, "They told me it will be like this."

God has promised to grant your expectations, whether good or bad. So, let your expectations be based on God's Word, for it is higher than any evil experience or information you may have had or heard about marriage (Proverbs 10:24).

If you are already married, there is still a chance to change all negative expectations. As a couple, discuss your positive expectations and I guarantee that things will work out more smoothly in your home.

Unmarried ladies and young men, what do you expect in marriage? Your expectations shall not be cut off! Before we got married, my husband and I made discoveries from God's Word that made us expect a hitch-free marriage. Till today, those expectations have not been cut off.

Become A Doer Of The Word

Every house is as strong as it's foundation. The blueprint is our expectation. The foundation is then laid according to the plan in the blueprint. If your expectation is to enjoy the honour in marriage, it follows that you will have to begin to do what makes for honour. The doing of the Word of God, is the laying of a foundation for a fulfilled family life.

Knowledge is in hearing; but it is mere information until it is put to practice. Simply knowing the Word of God is not enough, applying it is what makes it produces, for you (James. 1:22).

Just like a builder puts block upon block, you put line upon line, precept upon precept of God's Word into building your home.

When you have contacted God's Word for every part of your family, and begin to do it, there will be times when you will come face to face with challenges. At such times, sit down first and allow the Holy Spirit to quicken a scripture in your heart. The more of God's Word that is stored up in your heart, the more restful you will be. Then there will be no trouble you cannot triumph over, nor trial that will not become a testimony.

The process of building requires the counting of cost (Luke 14:28). There is a cost for peace, a cost for love, a cost for submission, a cost for fulfilment!

Before you quarrel with your spouse over any issue, count the cost of your actions and reactions. Many times when you are angry, you say things you later come to regret. But if you learn to count the cost of the words you speak, peace will rest in your home (Proverbs 15:1-2).

Operating In Wisdom (For Men)

There is nothing of beauty that didn't take some work to put in place. Just like every beautiful garden was tended before it became beautiful, and must continue to be tended if it must remain beautiful; in like manner, marriage must be tended before it can work, and must continue to be tended to continue working.

As a husband, the Bible instructs you to dwell with your wife according to knowledge. I like the way the Amplified version puts it:

> *In the same way you married men should live considerately with (your wives), with an intelligent recognition (of the marriage relation), honoring the woman as (physically) the weaker, but (realizing that you) are joint heirs of the grace (God's*

unmerited favor) of life, in order that your prayers may not be hindered and cut off. (Otherwise you cannot pray effectively.)

1 Peter 3:7 (Amp. Bible)

When a man understands the nature of his wife and works according to that understanding, problems are less likely to arise in their home. He puts less pressure on her, because he realises that she is not a robot. She is a wife, mother and homemaker all at once, and these all place a demand on her. He must be considerate of her feelings and needs, and be available to minister to her.

The second clause, **"giving honour unto the wife..."** implies that wives are not to be treated as slaves or inferior human beings, but are to be held in respect. Their views should be sought and they should be allowed to make their contributions in the home.

When a man beats his wife, he exhibits folly (Proverbs 26:4). No matter how provoked, a man must never stoop so low.

For no man ever yet hated his own flesh; but nourisheth and cherisheth it, even as the Lord the church.

Ephesians 5:29

Beating your wife is a sin against God. Being joined in holy wedlock, God sees the couple as one — that is why

He called the man and his wife "Adam" (Genesis 5:2). It was Adam who gave his wife a separate name, Eve.

Statistics have shown that more than 85 per cent of marriages in the West involved wife battering. Husband, don't turn your wife's body to a punching bag! Remember that her body is the temple of the Holy Spirit.

Lack of communication and understanding, among others, are some of the reasons some men abuse and beat their wives. The man must understand that the woman was given to him by God to take care of, not to beat.

Surprisingly, the role of the husband is drawn from that of Christ towards the Church, not from any human example. Thus, as we have mentioned earlier, the man must discover the selfless way Christ loved the Church and love his wife the same way, by God's grace.

Don't give up on your wife. Give her honour. Don't render evil for evil, don't seek to repay every wrong with a wrong, for two wrongs don't make a right. Jesus endured all contradictions of sinners. We too can overlook certain things just as He did.

Operating In Wisdom (For Women)

Every wise woman buildeth her house: but the foolish plucketh it down with her hands.

Proverbs 14:1

God, in His infinite wisdom, has planned one man for

one woman. Every woman in God's design has her own home. What becomes of that home, however, depends on the woman. This appears to be an awesome responsibility, but by the grace of God and hard work, it is accomplishable.

Abigail was a woman of wisdom, a woman with a good understanding.

> *Now the name of the man was Nabal; and the name of his wife Abigail; and she was a woman of good understanding...but the man was churlish and evil in his doings...*

1 Samuel 25:3

Abigail had made a mistake. The man she married was not what she expected. He was not a good man and they were definitely unequally yoked. Yet to have lived with him for all the years she did and got along without fighting or becoming like him in character, proved she was a woman of a wise heart. A time came when her churlish (bad mannered) husband provoked David. She mediated and saved her entire household and restrained David from avenging himself.

Wisdom is undoubtedly the principal thing.

Learn To Adapt

I believe one wise step Abigail took was to adapt to the

situation. Become adjusted to your husband's plans, way of life, etc. This does not mean when he is going wrong you leave him or follow his ways. It simply means to be flexible to his decisions.

...Married women...adapt yourselves to them...
1 Peter 3:1 (Amp. Bible)

When he takes decisions that are different from your plans, see how you can work them out and fit in. Remember that as a believer, all things will work out for good, but you must heed the Lord's instructions.

If he has certain weaknesses that you are strong in, help him; appreciate his good points, point out his mistakes in a kind and gentle way.

Embrace wisdom, it will bring you to honour, it will promote you from mediocrity to greatness. It will make your home precious before God and men. Inside wisdom is direction, because wisdom is knowing what to do next and having a sense of direction. That sense of direction leads you to a place of distinction, a place of glorification.

When you operate in wisdom, your home begins to shine as gold. People cannot help but be attracted to you, just as the glitter of gold attracts people.

...A man's wisdom maketh his face to shine...
Ecclesiastes 8:1

Knowing how to apply the knowledge of the Word of God, is wisdom. It will help you to know how to speak positive and edifying words to your spouse, relate with your in-laws in genuine love, etc. Wisdom is therefore, the principal thing for success in marriage.

8

Practice Hospitality!

Hospitality is the friendly, generous reception and entertainment of guests or strangers, especially in one's own home.

Being hospitable is very important in marriage. Let's examine a few of the benefits of hospitality:

Angelic Presence

> *Be not forgetful to entertain strangers: for thereby some have entertained angels unawares.*
>
> Hebrews 13:2

It is a known fact that where the angels of God are sent to minister to the heirs of salvation, they are there to defend you, provide for you and generally minister to you. So, as you are hospitable, you end up welcoming them into your home.

Abraham and Sarah for instance, entertained angels. They both made the visitors feel welcomed, relaxed and refreshed. By their hospitality, they received their son Isaac!

Increases

Whatever level you have attained in life, increase is still possible, and hospitality brings increases. Those who give never want. Their giving yields returns and comes back to them a hundred fold. Sometimes, hospitality may not be convenient, but as you sow in tears, God ensures that you reap in joy.

At Women fellowship meetings, I often encourage the women to always be hospitable, both at home and outside. One of the women testified of how a visitor came to their house and did not have enough money with which to return to his station. He belonged to another branch of the church. She told him her husband was out of town and the money he left wasn't even enough for them. She, however, sold some food stuff and gave him the money.

Before the man left, he made some prophetic utterances, that God would surprise her. From the following week, God began to visit their home with money, materials and foodstuff as never before! Where there was not enough previously, suddenly, their home became a place of abundance!

Hospitality brings honour and increase. The fear of being impoverished if you feed people, will become a thing of the past when you know that givers never lack; rather, you will always have more than enough to eat and to give out to others.

There is, however, a need for caution here. There are some wolves clothed in sheepskin. There is therefore, a need to exercise caution as you throw open your doors, for some use it as an occasion to do evil. Wisdom has to be applied here.

For singles, you can also be hospitable. Rebecca is a perfect example of hospitality. When Abraham's servant came to Mesopotamia to take a wife for Isaac, he said a prayer to God:

> *...Let it come to pass, that the damsel to whom I shall say, Let down thy pitcher, I pray thee, that I may drink; and she shall say, Drink, and I will give thy camels drink also: let the same be she that thou hast appointed for thy servant Isaac...*
>
> Genesis 24:14

The servant knowing the kind of family Isaac belonged to (a family addicted to hospitality), he prayed for a kind and hospitable wife for Isaac. He knew that any woman who would offer water to a stranger and his camels would be a hospitable person. The criteria for his choice was not possessions, height, beauty or education, but a warm, loving heart.

Singles who are hospitable will certainly welcome their life partners some way. Are you believing God for a life partner? How hospitable are you? May God give you understanding! The joy of having a life partner can be yours, if you will add a touch of friendliness and hospitality to your life.

If you are married, it is probable that it was your hospitable response to your spouse that drew the two of you together. No one marries an unapproachable, unloving, or unfriendly person. So, to continue to enjoy this honour and acceptance, you must continue to be hospitable.

Let Brotherly Love Continue

There is a catalyst that makes hospitality easy, it is called **brotherly love**. It is what makes you want to reach out to others and give them a helping hand. It is what makes you want to share what you have with others. Hospitality has great benefits, but brotherly love should be the reason for reaching out to others

(Romans 12:10,13).

Brotherly love can find expression through giving. It could be a cup of water, a meal, money, a warm smile or a listening ear, whatever is within your power to give. Don't eat all your food alone and drink all your water alone. Remember that the liberal soul shall be made fat (Proverbs 11:25)! Hospitality is not really in what is given, but in the way it is given.

Brotherly love should be what activates hospitality and not selfish gain. Philemon ensured that he refreshed the bowels of the saints, therefore he could be called a true brother. As Christians, we are all brothers since we have the same Father; except we relate with one another on the basis of love, we cannot please Him.

This was the strength of the first century Church. No one had a need. Those who had, eagerly distributed to others who had none; they had all things in common (Acts 2:44-45). As a result of this display of brotherly love, God's power was evident in their midst.

You must be sold out to hospitality; it is the path to God's presence in your marriage and home. You can make it a point of duty to bring great joy and consolation to members of the household of faith.

In the early days of ministry, my husband and I had to share our home and toilet facilities with the whole church. We did it then without grumbling or complaining, knowing that is was just a phase and we would pass through it to a better phase. I believe that was one of the reasons why God blessed us with a larger place.

We learnt early that a friendly and open home is commended by God. In our home, we are given to hospitality and we enjoy it. In actual fact, it is our watchword! Genuine and sincere hospitality brings with it great rewards. You will not miss your reward!

9

Family Finance

It is important to understand the place of money in marriage, to avoid tension.

For wisdom is a defence, and money is a defence...
Ecclesiastes 7:12

Money is simply a medium of exchange. It is required to live comfortably on the earth. It is a defence, because with it you are not embarrassed.

However, handling finances is a very sensitive area for couples. It is therefore crucial to say a few things about family finances here.

To the men: Right from the time God blessed Adam with a wife, he has been the head of the family. This also placed upon him the responsibility of providing for his household (1 Timothy 5:8).

So, by God's arrangement, the husband is to provide for his family. He is the one who must ensure there is food for members of his family. He must ensure his family members are well taken care of, especially his immediate family members (Song of Solomon 1:6). Therefore, the man must labour with his hands, especially as a married man; you cannot afford to be lazy. Your hands must be working hands. There is dignity in labour

> *Wealth gotten by vanity shall be diminished: but he that gathereth by labour shall increase.*
>
> Proverbs 13:11

God is serious about the need for men to rise up to their God-given roles, even in this day and age where women also work to help make ends meet. A man who is too slothful to find gainful employment should not eat.

> *For even when we were with you, this we commanded you, that if any would not work, neither should he eat.*
>
> 2 Thessalonians 3:10

The man is responsible for catering for his wife and children. If he fails in this duty, he is a failure indeed! It is a curse for the wife to take on this responsibility.

To the women: Everything she has belongs to her husband, even her income. If she is employed outside the home, she must submit **all** to him. This does not mean that she may not have her own separate account, if they both agree to this. But by divine order, this account also belongs to him.

There should be no "his" and "hers" in family finance. Both should have access to each other's money. Where there's a joint account, no one should spend money without informing the other. At an agreed date, both partners can come together to plan the family budget, mapping out how much should be spent on food, children and each other, as well as paying electricity bills, etc. It is refusing to work together as a team that places families under tension.

Trust is the key word in family finance. Husband and wife must trust each other enough to put their money together, and be prudent in spending it. Note that accountability helps to boost trust. Where no one wants to be accountable to the other, there will be no progress financially. The virtuous woman in Proverbs 31 is trustworthy.

The heart of her husband doth safely trust in her...
Verse 11

You can earn each other's trust, causing your hearts to be perfectly at rest. A man cannot win his wife's trust, if he selfishly spends all the money on new clothes and the likes on himself. His wife might also begin to sneak out money from the feeding money to buy her personal things.

A good place to start in building up trust in one another, is by being open about your monthly income. If you lie about it, you are only opening the way for the enemy.

A man shouldn't shift the responsibility of handling family finances to the woman alone. He may assign a portion of it to her, but should not abandon his responsibility and then turn around to blame her half way through the month, if the money is not sufficient.

Giving

Love is...never...selfish...

1 Corinthians 13:5 (TLB)

God so loved the world, He gave. He demonstrated His love for man by taking the initiative and giving us His Son, even when no man understood what He was doing and could not say, "Thank you". It was in His selfless giving that the world was won. If man and wife will learn to prefer each other in love, consider and think of ways to bless the other, family life will be so much sweeter.

God is a giving God. Giving is godlike. If we claim to be God's children, you must imitate Him in all things.

Beloved, let us love one another: for love is of God;

and every one that loveth is born of God, and knoweth God.

1 John 4:7

Giving gifts to one another spices up the marriage. You can take the initiative to surprise your partner with thoughtful little gifts. If it did wonders for you during your courtship days, it will do you no harm to carry the habit over into marriage.

Giving To God

The Bible declares that two is better than one. You can "better" your giving to the Lord by giving as a family, thus making better your receiving (Luke 6:38). You must encourage each other to sow seeds. Though hard times have come upon the earth, you will be exempted as you purpose to keep sowing into the Kingdom.

As a family, ensure your tithe is paid, either separately as husband, wife and children or together as a family. Give offerings according to your size also. Don't rob God in your offerings. Ensure that your children also give offerings.

It is wisdom to sow to the kingdom, even when you need every penny. There is a portion to eat and a portion to sow (Proverbs 11:24).

Giving To The Poor

You must be generous to the poor, underprivileged and those who do not have as much as you have. God loves the merciful and releases blessings upon him.

> *He that giveth unto the poor shall not lack: but he that hideth his eyes shall have many a curse.*
>
> Proverbs 28:27

When you reach out to bless the poor, God ensures that you do not lack. Anyone who pretends not to know those who are in need is selfish and will incur a curse upon himself.

Cornelius was a man given to almsgiving. One day, God visited him and blessed him with salvation. You, too, can register in God's book of remembrance by being open and generous. Women can emulate the virtuous woman in Proverbs 31.

Giving To Men Of God

As couples, you must provoke each other to do right things. Sowing to the men of God placed over us is right, and provokes great blessings from the Lord. God is glorified when you handle your money this way.

Money is actually limited in value except it is placed in the hands of God. It has wings. If you don't send it on errand, someday it will take up wings and fly away by itself.

> *Wilt thou set thine eyes upon that which is not? for riches certainly make themselves wings; they fly away as an eagle toward heaven.*
>
> Proverbs 23:5

Money is a god, it seeks to be worshipped. That is why Matthew 6:24 says you cannot serve God and mammon. "Mammon" means money. It is a good servant but a terrible master; don't allow the absence of it determine the atmosphere of your home. There are some people once they are angry you know there is no money in their pocket. Don't let it destroy the peace and joy in your home.

Some serve money and give it the place that only God should occupy in their lives. But when you dispose of your money in the above listed ways, you are serving God with it, and is an evidence of your love for Him and your liberality. Money then cannot be your god.

However, you worship money when you clutch on to it, refusing to disperse it, and gathering it for selfish purposes. Those who run after money are running after sorrow. My husband often says, "If you run after money you will mourn." So, run after God, and money will run after you. Whatever comes your way financially, learn to put God first, separating the first fruits of harvest unto Him.

Giving To Parents

Many marriages are in a financial mess because they fail in their covenant responsibilities to their parents

Children, obey your parents in the Lord: for this is right.

Honour thy father and mother; which is the first commandment with promise;

That it may be well with thee, and thou mayest live long on the earth.

Ephesians 6:1-3

We have an undeniable responsibility towards our parents. It is your duty to honour your parents according to how God has blessed you. You can't have parents who don't have food to eat and you are wasting food in your house. That is irresponsibility. You must honour your parents, if life must be well with you.

10

The Works Of The Flesh

There is a war that rages within, the battle goes on everyday. Sometimes, one party gains the upper hand, another time the other party sings a victory song. As long as we are in this temple of clay, the battle lines are drawn.

Apostle Paul was no stranger to this type of battle. It raged on continually within him until he cried out:

...I do what I don't want to — what I hate...It seems to be a fact of life that when I want to do what is right, I inevitably do what is wrong ... My new life tells me to do right, but the old nature that is still inside me loves to sin ... Who will free me from my slavery to this deadly lower nature? Thank God! It has been done by Jesus Christ our Lord. He has set me free.

Romans 7:15-25 (TLB)

Paul was describing the age-old war between the flesh and the new nature. When God created man, He put into him the human nature. That is, the ability to feel, have desires, aim at targets or goals; these are what make us human. That nature was pure, because it worked in consonance with the spiritman, which was in tune with God. The desires were godly and pure.

Then man fell and this nature became corrupted. The sin nature now became dominant, until Christ came! Then as many as received Him, He gave power to subdue the old sin nature. He did not destroy it, for it is still very much within us, at war with the new nature; but He gave us the power of choice, the ability to yield to the dictates of the flesh or the spirit.

Let not sin therefore reign in your mortal body ... to whom ye yield yourselves servants to obey, his servants ye are...whether of sin unto death, or of obedience unto righteousness.

Romans 6:12,16

By the victory of the Lord Jesus Christ at Calvary, we are without excuse. If we yield to the flesh we shall reap corruption and death; but if we yield to the spirit, we reap life! It is a matter of choice(Galatians 6:8).

Marriage does not automatically lift a man above the works of the flesh. Yielding to the flesh accounts for the heartache many born-again couples are still experiencing in their homes today. What are these works?

> *...impure thoughts, eagerness for lustful pleasure, idolatry, spiritism...hatred and fighting, jealousy and anger, constant effort to get the best for yourself, complaints and criticisms, the feeling that everyone else is wrong except those in your own little group...*
> Galatians 5:19-20 (TLB)

Let's find out how a few vices can steal peace and joy from marriage and how to combat them.

Slothfulness

Laziness is a work of the flesh. Good homes and marriages don't just drop from heaven, they are made to happen. God had to first work for six days, creating the world before He rested (Genesis 2:2). You must be ready to do what it takes, before you can enjoy rest, peace and honour in your marriage.

If there is any indication of laziness or slothfulness in you, get rid of it now, because the fruit of laziness is shame, whether it is spiritual (laziness in studying the Word of God, prayers) or physical (doing household chores or caring for the family) (Proverbs 10:5). Nobody loves a lazy person.

A brother who read one of my tracts titled, **Created To**

Create, said, *"I was very happy when I read your tract. I am in business now. But I used to be very lazy, right from my youth, to the point that I was always late to school because of oversleeping. But after reading your tract, which mentioned a sister that decided to sell boiled water for drinking in school and prospered by it, and another lady youth corps member who sold tomatoes in Kaduna and bought a car with the profits, I became ashamed of myself, because my business was not prospering due to my lazy attitude.*

I was then challenged to change my lazy ways and decided to act according to your advice in that tract. God touched my soul and I was converted. I thank God for opening my eyes. My life and my business are no more the same!"

Slothfulness is a destroyer of families. Many know what to do to improve the state of their families, but they simply won't do it or they do it for a while and give up. You must co-operate with God for your marriage to work.

There are many things you have read about in God's Word and other inspired books. If you will only do half of what you have heard and claim to know, honour will undeniably be yours. Remember, wisdom is not in the accumulation of knowledge, but in its application.

Receive grace to be diligent, so you can enjoy your marriage, in Jesus' name!

Idolatry

God commanded man:

> **Thou shalt have no other gods before me.**
>
> Exodus 20:3

Nothing should come before your relationship with God, whether it be a car, jewelry, children, or even your spouse. Your love for God should not be replaced with a love for money, shoes or any other thing.

> **...Thou shalt love the Lord thy God with all thy heart, and with all thy soul, and with all thy mind.**
>
> Matthew 22:37

There is another dimension to idolatry. The Bible says:

> **...Stubbornness is as iniquity and idolatry...**
>
> 1 Samuel 15:23

Stubbornness is equated with idolatry. This means that before God, stubbornness is a grievous sin as the worship of graven images! What does it mean to be stubborn? It means to be adamant, to be fixed in purpose or opinion. To refuse positive changes. God hates it!

Saul's Kingdom was cut off from him because he refused correction. In your family life also, stubbornness can be destructive. The man makes up his mind to do something and refuses to be swayed by the pleadings of his wife, even when her reasons are obviously genuine. He refuses even to consider her point. Such men end up in big trouble.

He, that being often reproved hardeneth his neck, shall suddenly be destroyed, and that without remedy.

Proverbs 29:1

Whosoever is stubborn (whether husband or wife) will end up being stripped of honour. It is like breaking the hedge, anything can happen. Wives must be submissive to their husbands, leaving every final decision making or approval to the head of the home. Any woman who is strong-willed and unbending, is signing up for disgrace and destruction. As a Christian woman, you must work on letting the fruit of the spirit, such as gentleness replace stubbornness.

A sister was upset by her husband and angrily decided to leave her home. The man and many other people pleaded with her to return home, but due to stubbornness, she refused, taking advantage of the fact that since he is a Christian he could not look unto another woman. After a few months, her husband stopped asking for her return, she then decided to go back home. But to her surprise, it was too late! Her husband too, deciding to do his own thing, had looked for someone else! Alas, even though they were both believers, they were robbed of a successful marriage due to stubbornness.

Flee stubbornness! Be flexible with your spouse. Allow mercy and compassion, and God will not let you experience shame in your home.

Anger

We all get angry at one time or the other, but the difference between this and the work of the flesh is sin.

> *Be ye angry, and sin not: let not the sun go down upon your wrath.*
>
> *Ephesians 4:26*

I like the way The Living Bible puts it:

> *If you are angry, don't sin by nursing your grudge. Don't let the sun go down with you still angry get over it quickly;*
>
> *For when you are angry you give a mighty foothold to the devil.*
>
> Ephesians 4:26-27

By holding on to anger, you open the door to sin. If you get upset about the way your spouse does certain things at certain times, rather than exploding and speaking cruel words which can cause irreparable damage, control your emotions and take a walk or go to the prayer closet, until your anger simmers down.

It is like a kettle of boiling water. As long as the fire is on, the water boils hotter. To cool the water, you would need to turn off the source of fire, place the kettle on a cool surface and give it time to cool down. Within a few hours, that formerly boiling water can be drunk straight from a glass. Anger is just like that.

Some people try to suppress anger. They get angry, but they swallow it, pretend everything is all right and plaster a smile on their faces. They are like hot bottles of Coca-Cola, shaken. Once the lid is opened the hot liquid rushes out in torrents. Bottling up anger is risky, and an explosion is only a matter of time.

You can let off steam by discussing the issue at an appropriate time. In a situation where you cannot speak out immediately, you can run into your prayer closet, tell God exactly how you feel, and let Him speak peace to you. Anger is a killer. Simeon and Levi who slew the men of Shechem because of their uncontrollable anger, got a horrible sentence:

Simeon and Levi are brethren... Cursed be their anger, for it was fierce; and their wrath, for it was cruel: I will divide them in Jacob, and scatter them in Israel.

Genesis 49:5,7

Anger must be dealt with, if you want to avoid the shame that division and scattering bring to a marriage. Anger puts asunder faster than fornication. One may not kill physically, yet by angry words or even silence, you can kill a person's spirit!

...I say unto you, That whosoever is angry with his brother without a cause shall be in danger of the judgment...

Matthew 5:22

Anger has the same consequences as murder. Learn to control yourself!

Complaints And Criticisms

The secrets of living a life void of complaints are thanksgiving and appreciation. Even when you have a genuine reason to do so, complaining is not the right way of making a case. Complaining displeases God. He hates it! My husband says every complaint complicates issues for you.

Those who complain are those who focus on the things that have not been done, choosing to forget the ones that have been done. They are people who look back in self pity, instead of looking ahead to a bright and colourful future.

Complaints and criticisms were what got the natural Israel into a lot of trouble in the wilderness. Their case was genuine — the Red Sea ahead, the host of Egypt behind; but they chose the wrong medium of getting God to intervene. When they got to the brink of the promised land, they again accepted the evil report of the 10 spies and murmured again. This time, God did not spare them (Numbers 14:26-39).

Your marriage and home will be more pleasant and peaceful, without complaints and wicked criticisms. There is nothing wrong with corrective criticisms, it helps to balance us up. For instance, if your wife wears a dress that you think does not complement her and she asks, "How do I look?" expecting wonderful comments, and you say, "Well, I think you'll look better in something else." That's a criticism, but one from a positive angle.

A critic is one who points out faults. No one should assume the role of a critic, but we need to be available to point out what is not right about our mates, with a view to rendering help and effecting positive changes. There are many ways to do this without turning into a fault-finder or a perfectionist.

There is that speaketh like the piercings of a sword:

but the tongue of the wise is health.

Proverbs 12:18

In summary, let me reiterate that the flesh refers to the old sin nature. It is the human nature given to man and intended for the greater glory of God, but was corrupted as a result of the fall. For instance, human instinct to eat, sleep or perhaps have sexual relation becomes the works of the flesh when not controlled.

When in excess, eating is gluttony, sleeping is slothfulness and sex, perversion. With the coming of Jesus, we said earlier, sin no longer has dominion over us (Romans 6:14). Sin is sin, no matter the size. Many think only sexual sins are grievous, but all sins stink before God. It is time to put off *"the garment spotted by the flesh."*

Keys To Triumph Over The Flesh

Prayer And Fasting

When Jesus taught His disciples to pray, the two words that opened the prayer were, **"Our Father."** God is our Father if we are born-again Christians. Therefore, we can boldly approach His throne of grace to obtain grace to live victoriously over the works of the flesh. Ask, and you will receive.

Secondly, for every work of the flesh, there is a fruit of the Spirit to turn it around for good. Engaging in Word-based prayer or supplication is one sure way to free oneself from the entanglements of the flesh.

Do you have a problem with lust? Pick up your Bible, a concordance, a biro and note book. Write out the scripture verses that discuss lust and its consequences, then go to God in prayer, breaking the yoke of lust over your life, and close with thanksgiving, knowing that God has answered you already.

Fasting means abstinence from food in order to do spiritual business. Engage in a fast as you pray and study the Word. Making heaven is well worth the sacrifice (I Corinthians 9:27).

Praying in tongues is also one sure way to build up your inner man. Inner strength and character are needed, if we are to resist various temptations and urges of the flesh.

> *...Building up yourselves...praying in the Holy Ghost.*
>
> Jude 20

The Word Of God

The Psalmist said:

> *Thy word have I hid in mine heart, that I might not*

sin against thee.

Psalm 119:11

David had fallen once to adultery. He didn't want to fall again. So, he picked up the Word of God, and by constant study and meditation, hid the Word in his heart.

As we get attached to the Word, our minds are renewed and we will live continually in victory over the works of the flesh.

Confessing The Word Of God

The Word of God must be confessed daily. Upon waking up each day, you can go ahead to start declaring: *"Sin shall not have dominion over me: for I am not under the law, but under grace."*

The spoken word has tremendous power. As it is uttered, "worlds" are either framed or destroyed. You will see more on this in the next chapter.

The Word of God must be meditated upon, for it to become an integral part of our lives.

Word Application

A conscious effort must be made to walk in line with the Word. That is, to apply what you read. The Word is quick and powerful, that is true; but it must be put to work to exhibit those qualities. If you are a man or woman who wants to learn to subdue the flesh, keep your eyes from looking lustfully after a woman or people of the opposite sex. Stop reading pornographic materials, the spirit behind them are destructive. Don't keep wrong company and God's Word will work for you. Are you given to anger? Subdue it by confessing the Word and shutting up your mouth when provoked.

But be ye doers of the word, and not hearers only...
James 1:22

11

The Power Of The Tongue

For in many things we offend all. If any man offend not in word, the same is a perfect man, and able also to bridle the whole body.

James 3:2

What would constitute a perfect marriage according to this scripture? A perfect tongue! What is a perfect tongue? It is a tongue that selects what it says and one which speaks the truth of God's Word, rather than the negative facts of life.

What man is he that desireth life, and loveth many days, that he may see good?

Keep thy tongue from evil, and thy lips from speaking guile.

Psalm 34:12-13

God has promised to grant the desires of your heart.

So, say only what you want to have. You may desire life, but if you permit your tongue to speak death, you cannot have anything but death. Why?

> *...He shall have whatsoever he saith.*
>
> Mark 11:23

God wanted to create a world that would be very good. His desire was implanted deep in His heart. The day He gave voice to His desire, our world was born. When He looked at all He had made, He put a final stamp of approval and declared, *"Very good"* (Genesis 1:31). Even if the creation work was just good, as soon as God proclaimed that it was very good, the earth adjusted. There were no thorns, no thistles, no violence, no death; those were not part of the arrangement. It was disobedience that brought poverty, sickness and death.

Whatever good you desire to see in your family, speak it into being. You have spoken enough negative things. You have spoken out of the information your mind has stored up for years. But the same mouth that has spoken the facts of life can speak the truth of the Word.

If your marriage is good, it can be better; there is still room for perfection!

Comparing the tongue to the rudder of a ship, we discover that it controls the entire system. Therefore, if the tongue is tamed by the Word of God, the body will move in the direction of the Word.

For instance, children who are not doing well in school, can be redirected by the correct use of the tongue. By acceptance and positive reinforcement, the child discovers his abilities and develops them. You will begin to experience perfection in your homes, when you say what you desire to see.

Apostle Paul was aboard a ship. He had counselled the captain in charge to delay their trip, but he did not. A time came when a tempestuous wind rose against them. Later Paul stood and declared that no life would be lost. An angel had disclosed this to him previously. Until he spoke, the angel had nothing to work with. Apostle Paul needed to establish it by saying it (Acts 27:25).

Paul was working on one principle:

> *...As truly as I live, saith the Lord, as ye have spoken in mine ears, so will I do to you.*
>
> Numbers 14:28

If Paul could by the confession of his mouth save the lives of all on board the ship, you can save your marriage by the words of your mouth. Husbands can have the type of wives, they desire by calling those things which be not, as though they were. You want a submissive wife? Then say, "Oh I thank God for you Judith (or whatever her name is). You are so submissive, so caring. I appreciate you." She will soon be meek and submissive, because her man has learnt to use his words correctly.

God had perfect control over His tongue and the use of His mouth. He always said what He meant and meant what He said; so He always had perfect results. When you do as your Father did, you will have what He has. Perfect men constitute perfect marriages, and a perfect man is one who controls his tongue.

Turn Around

> *Behold, we put bits in the horses' mouths, that they may obey us; and we turn about their whole body.*
>
> James 3:3

If by putting bits in the horse's mouth you successfully turn it in the direction you want, it follows that there is what to put in your mouth, to turn your family from grass to grace. It is God's Word!

Hannah wanted a turn around from barrenness to fruitfulness, and she secured it with her tongue. She discovered that weeping was not the solution, so she voiced out her desire.

> *And she vowed a vow, and said, O Lord of hosts, if thou wilt...give unto thine handmaid a man child,*

then I will give him unto the Lord...

1 Samuel 1:11

People are confronted with all manner of challenges, but because they haven't opened their mouths to voice out their petition, it remains. Hannah was confronted with the reproach of barrenness in her family life. But as she spoke out, the mountain bowed.

> *For verily I say unto you, That whosoever shall say unto this mountain, Be thou removed, and be thou cast into the sea; and shall not doubt in his heart, but shall believe that those things which he saith shall come to pass; he shall have whatsoever he saith.*
>
> Mark 11:23

Mountains are adamant; they require constant faith "pressure" to move them. They may refuse to move at first, but you must refuse to be moved. As you stand your ground, they will move. United, a husband and wife can level financial mountains, mountains of barrenness and any other type of mountain they may be confronted with. But they must keep speaking the Word till it moves.

Esther had an unbelieving husband, but by the wise use of her tongue, she won his favour for her people. Every man can be won by his wife, but her behaviour and speech will either hasten a turnaround or put it off

(I Peter 3:1). God is available to turn your situations around; but He won't speak to those situations for you, you must do that by yourself.

Your tongue was not designed for murmuring, complaining or uttering careless words; it was created for appreciating God.

For the right use of his tongue, Hezekiah had 15 more years added to him (Isaiah 38:1-6)! Many years are subtracted from some people's lives because they speak death instead of life. Many marriages suffer crash-landings shortly after takeoff, because of the wrong use of the tongue. But no matter how bad your spouse is, he or she can change, if your tongue utters only positive words. Words can change the destiny of men.

"...Whithersoever The Governor Listeth..."

We see another mystery in James 3:4:

> *Behold also the ships, which though they be so great...yet are they turned about...whithersoever the governor listeth.Behold also the ships, which though they be so great...yet are they turned about...whithersoever the governor listeth.*

If every ship has a governor, then you are the governor of your life. It is the governor who decides the direction to which the ship will sail. You decide the direction your marriage will take by your choice of words. Everyone who turned their destinies around did so, by the right use of their tongue. Jabez is a good example (1 Chronicles 4:10).

Some speak facts of life — the woes of the world, the famine in so and so part of the world, the killings in the south, etc. They say everything but God's Word. You must accept responsibility over your home and marriage! By God's design, your marriage is destined to be bright and full of pleasure, but you can alter that by your utterances.

Joshua and Caleb were among the twelve spies sent to spy out the Promised Land. Ten verbalised what they saw with their eyes and thought in their hearts. But not so with Joshua and Caleb, who saw what the others saw, but said what they believed God would do.

> *...They are bread for us: their defence is departed from them, and the Lord is with us: fear them not.*
>
> Numbers14:9

God cannot turn your captivity until you change your words, and your words cannot change positively until you are of another spirit. The tree determines the fruit, and the governor, the course of the ship.

How Great A Matter A Little Fire Kindleth

Even so the tongue is a little member, and boasteth great things. Behold, how great a matter a little fire kindleth!

James 3:5

Fires are often started by the strike of a match. The size of the match cannot be compared with the size of the fire it sparked off. The tongue is a small member, yet many fires in the family which have caused so much destruction are traceable to it. If there is anything that destroys homes and families, it is the unkempt tongue and the unguided mouth.

Sometimes in the heat of anger, things you would never dream of saying are said. Quarrels and strifes are products of a loose tongue. Miriam and Aaron used their tongues against Moses and procured leprosy for Miriam.

If you do not control what you say to and about each other as couples, you will reap shame instead of glory. If Moses had not intervened and pleaded with God on Miriam's behalf, she would have been a leper for life.

The unbridled tongue and unguided mouth are the reasons for the leprosy of fighting, malice, discord, fornication, adultery, etc, in many homes and families today.

You can purpose to speak what is "good to the use of edifying, that it may minister grace unto the hearers" (Ephesians 4:29). You will become the proverbial fountain sending forth bitter and sweet water from the same place, if you use your mouth both to bless and to curse.

Taming the Tongue

> *But the tongue can no man tame; it is an unruly evil, full of deadly poison.*
>
> James 3:8

By *"can no man tame"*, God does not exempt us from taking responsibilities over the use of our tongue. What it means is that the natural man cannot tame the tongue, only the supernatural man can. "How?,"you may ask.

The following is a guide:

Feeding On The Word

The Word of God is the food of the spirit-man, as bread is to the body.

When the body eats nutritionally balanced meals, it grows strong and is able to resist common diseases. In like manner, when your spirit-man feeds well on the

Word, it becomes strong and is able to control the tongue. The tongue speaks out what is in the heart. If garbage is in the heart, garbage will come out from the tongue.

The mind is like a sponge. It soaks up what it gets from the written pages, the television, radio, etc. But when it comes in contact with the Word of God, there must be a squeezing out of the junk and a soaking up of the Word.

> *...For out of the abundance of the heart the mouth speaketh.*
>
> Matthew 12:34

When you are full of the Word of God, the moment you are confronted with a situation, the abundance that is in you will flow out. When a man speaks negatively always, the problem is with his heart.

Praying In The Spirit

You also build up yourself by praying in the spirit (Jude 20). The Holy Ghost is within you to help you deal with your weaknesses. As you speak in His language, you sanctify your speech and keep your tongue in check. This, however, calls for discipline. You must desire a change, then discipline yourself to keep in touch with the Holy Ghost. He is a gentle Spirit, and will not force Himself on you.

Set a watch, O Lord, before my mouth; keep the door of my lips.

Psalm 141:3

My husband would always say, "Keep your heart with all diligence, and your tongue with all discipline." The Holy Spirit will empower you to do this.

Do Battle With The Blood

When evil thoughts spring up within, you can plead the blood against them. Your mind does not belong to the enemy, so you must fight him with a weapon he knows and respects.

And they overcame him by the blood of the Lamb, and by the word of their testimony; and they loved not their lives unto the death.

Revelation 12:11

The Blood of Jesus is very powerful; your salvation was procured by it. If it was strong enough to purchase you from the enemy, then it is strong enough to keep your mind from demonic oppressions. So engage it.

Other Weapons

You can drink the Blood and eat the Body of Jesus in **the communion**, to keep your mouth speaking God's Word always. Confessing the Word daily will also help to tame the tongue.

These weapons are readily available and they help us keep our hearts and tongues. For more light on the communion, read my book, *The Communion Table*.

The anointing oil is another weapon that can be employed here, as yokes are destroyed by the anointing (Isaiah 10:27). If evil speaking has become a way of life with you, it is a yoke upon your neck. Break free by the anointing.

12

Beware Of Covetousness!

Many people are not satisfied with what they have per time. Nothing is ever enough, they always want more. Their lack of contentment gets them scheming and planning to collect what rightfully belongs to others.

Covetousness is a strong urge or desire to possess something, especially something that someone else has. You see something on someone and "**claim**"it, all in the name of faith. That's not faith, that's covetousness!

And having food and raiment, let us be therewith content.

1 Timothy 6:8

God urges us to mix godliness with contentment, especially in our homes. But some will not heed this admonition.

151

But godliness with contentment is great gain.

For we brought nothing into this world, and it is certain we can carry nothing out.

1 Timothy 6:6-7

Discontentment is what drives people into covetousness. Many believers are not demon-possessed as it were, but open the door to demonic influences by being "possession - possessed".

There is great gain in contentment. A man's life does not consist in the abundance of his possessions. Life means much more.

...Take heed, and beware of covetousness: for a man's life consisteth not in the abundance of the things which he possesseth.

Luke 12:15

You must learn to put possessions where they rightly belong. Anything that takes the place of God is idolatry.

Contentment brings peace of mind. I tell my children that anything we don't have in our home, we don't need. If it comes, fine; but I refuse to be possessed by possessions. Material things come and go. Whatever you have, make available to God and lay up treasures for yourself in heaven (Matthew 6:20-21). "Don't die for things, they are traps", my husband often says.

Where is your affection? Where is your heart? On God or on things? Where your treasure is determines where your heart will be. Life is in phases and men are in sizes. The greatest mistake a man can make is to overestimate himself. Everyone must realise that there are phases in life. Agree with the phase-by-phase lifting of God in your life.

Don't live above your level per time. Covetousness is a sin. It has destroyed and destabilized many homes! It is the devil's trap. As a family, eat your size per time, drink your size per time, sleep your size per time and wear your size per time. As covenant people, be assured of the fact that where you are today is the least place you will ever be. Your path is destined to shine brighter and brighter every passing day, until you get to God's ultimate for your life (Proverbs 4:18). However, you must accept the place you are now, knowing that:

> **Better is the end of a thing than the beginning thereof: and the patient in spirit than the proud in spirit.**
>
> Ecclesiastes 7:8

If you know that where you are going or heading for as a believer is better than where you are at present, you will be excited at your today. Colourful and bright is your future, you will get there. Some people refuse to accept their present positions, so they steal and cheat to have more.

Some singles base their choice of a life partner on the abundance of things the man has. Marriage that is founded on material possessions is on a shaky foundation. It soon falls apart. We must not be blinded by things, as life is much more than that.

> *Though thy beginning was small, yet thy latter end should greatly increase.*
>
> Job 8:7

Covetousness has driven some to the evil of comparing their spouses with others. They are not content with their own husbands or wives, rather Mr./Mrs. X's wife/ husband is better than their own. This is how coveting another person's spouse begins.

Nobody climbs a ladder from the top. Rung by rung you climb up, until you get to the top. Your future is bright, do not despise it like Esau, and eat your tomorrow today. Later, he sought for his inheritance with tears, but it was lost eternally (Hebrews 12:16-17). It was too late for Esau, may it not be too late for you!

People who want a ready- made life end up in ready- made troubles. My husband and I also had to start out at the first rung of the ladder in marriage and ministry, many times eating beans and gari (fermented cassava flakes) for supper, so we wouldn't need breakfast the next day. Some other times we didn't know where and when the next meal was coming from! But God has always been very faithful. We're not at that point anymore.

Material things come and go. You cannot afford to tie your life to them. Your focus must be on God, and when He becomes your focus, everything else loses value to you and yet you have more than enough!

Wrong Company

When you walk with covetous people, you will be like them. You must be particular about your choice of friends. You are either made or broken by friends. Covetousness is contagious.

The question therefore is, "Who is your friend?" My husband would say, "Show me your friend and I will show you who you are, for two cannot walk together except they be agreed" (Amos 3:3).

A materialistic person loses out on the joy of living, for all he thinks about is himself, not how to reach out to others. Remember, stagnant water stinks.

Husbands and wives are to be each other's best friend. That way, you can help your spouse when the love for things begins to draw him or her.

A covetous person cannot inherit the kingdom (1 Corinthians 6:9-10). Don't lose eternity to covetousness.

If God has given us all things that make living comfortable (2 Peter 1:3), why crave for more? When you choose the path of covetousness, you join company with Satan. He was not satisfied with his position; he wanted what was God's. Just as he cannot inherit the Kingdom of God, no one who follows his example will (Ephesians 5:5).

Having your eyes fixed on material things will also cause you to lose out on God's placement for you. God who sees the heart will refuse to appoint such a man. Gehazi lost his place to covetousness. He also might have ended up receiving a double portion of Elisha's spirit, but he lost it to covetousness. He wanted possessions at all cost before God provided them for him.

Times have changed, but the penalty for covetousness has not. Gehazi became an object of shame and reproach. The price of covetousness far outweighs the "gains". It can cost you your family! Achan lost out on God's best, and brought calamity upon his family (Joshua 7:24-26).

Also, anyone who embraces covetousness is shortening his days (Proverbs 28:16). Ananias and Sapphira cut short their days and brought calamity to their family because they were covetous. A man who is never satisfied with what he has per time, will run into dubious people and do some criminal things.

Let's go for God, then gold will go for us! God, in His mercy has designed an antidote for covetousness, it is His Word.

Incline my heart unto thy testimonies, and not to covetousness.

Turn away mine eyes from beholding vanity; and quicken thou me in thy way.

Psalm 119:36-37

If you keep your eyes from beholding, that is, being absorbed with things, you will deliver yourself from covetousness. If you keep your heart fixed on God, you deliver yourself from the encroachment of a materialistic world. You can keep yourself and your family from covetousness. God has given you power to live above it, you must turn your eyes away from its allure!

13

Beware Of
Unforgiveness!

Forgiveness simply means to decide not to punish someone for a wrong, to cancel debts owed. Forgiveness is a character trait of God. He is all-forgiving.

To the Lord our God belongs mercies and forgiveness, though we have rebelled against him.

Daniel 9:9

Ever since Adam, man has lived in rebellion to the Almighty God. Yet, because of His mercies, God has always pardoned our iniquities, the ultimate being the price paid at Calvary — Jesus Himself nailed to the cross, not for anything He did, but for our sins. Yet He cried out:

...Father, forgive them; for they know not what they do...

Luke 23:34

Unforgiveness has caused a lot of trouble in families. In most cases, it is the hidden factor behind separation and divorce. It is refusing to pardon something one's spouse or member of family has done.

Jesus never did any wrong. If anything, He was goodness Himself. Yet, they took Him and nailed Him to the cross of criminals. It is like the story narrated in Matthew 18:23-35. God, like the King in that parable, has forgiven us of so much evil, debts worth more than billions of pounds. If God could wipe away so much from our record, we must in turn be determined to demonstrate forgiveness to our spouses and family members.

There was a lady who after a decade of marriage decided that her marriage was a thorn in her flesh. She packed out of her home and filed for a divorce. However, in the process she got born again and after reading my book, *Marriage Covenant*, and some other anointed books, she discovered she had been living in self-righteousness and unforgiveness towards her husband. After this discovery, she forgave him and God miraculously healed her marriage. In her own words, she is having a honeymoon now. Honour and joy were restored once more.

What makes God forgive? I believe that aside from forgiveness coming out of His merciful nature, the sacrificial death of Jesus also cause Him to forgive. He looks back at the cross and remembers how much Jesus suffered for our iniquities, He sees the shed blood and it moves Him to forgive.

If we are to forgive each other, then we must be prepared to exercise patience:patience with the other person, because God is not through with working on us as individuals.

And be ye kind one to another, tender-hearted, forgiving one another, even as God for Christ's sake hath forgiven us.

Ephesians 4:32

We must be tender-hearted towards each other, soft, accommodating, easy to pardon and to show mercy. Some people can be so hard, unbending and uncompromising. Their mates commit little offences for which they will never be forgiven. Years after, they still hold on tight to that grudge, so bitterness creeps in. Wives and children are the greatest offenders here. We must be tender-hearted one towards another, ready to forgive absolutely as Christ did.

Many people are well dressed outside but inside are a bundle of rottenness because of bitterness. Young lady, you claim to have been abused in your youth by a relative, yes. But that is no reason for unforgiveness. Let go that bitterness, and let the balm in Gilead heal your wounds (Jeremiah 8:22). It is not just to forgive but to learn the secret of forgiving instantly. Never go to bed with a grudge, or else you may have bad dreams and nightmares.

Forgiveness liberates, it frees from the clutches of bitterness. Bitterness causes one to fail of the grace of God (Hebrews 12:15). You need that grace to make your home a haven of joy and honour. So, steer clear of unforgiveness, even if you have been wronged.

A man sick of the palsy was brought to Jesus. Jesus looking at Him said the unusual,

> *...Son, be of good cheer; thy sins be forgiven thee.*
>
> Matthew 9:2

The forgiveness of his sins preceded his healing. I believe that if we learn to forgive completely, we will experience healing from all manner of afflictions. A pastor's wife hearing this at a *Family Life Seminar*, decided to forgive her husband of whatever it was she claimed he had done. Previously she had been very sickly. When she decided to forgive him, however, she was miraculously healed! In addition to this miracle healing, she discovered that for once in their married life, they were able to make ends meet financially. Unforgiveness brings torment. It leads to affliction. It troubles people.

If God has forgiven us so much, the least we can do is to be ready to forgive the trespasses of our spouses, children, in-laws, and fellow Christians. No matter how much someone has offended you, even if it is so many times in a day, be prepared to forgive him. Do not pretend to be happy when you are hurt. Speak out your grievances and let the matter end there.

Outcome Of Unforgiveness

And his lord was wroth, and delivered him to the tormentors, till he should pay all that was due unto him.

So likewise shall my heavenly Father do also unto you, if ye from your hearts forgive not every one his brother their trespasses.

Matthew 18: 34-35

You incur the wrath of God when you refuse to forgive. If God is angry with you, who will defend you? The reason some people are going through untold hardships in life is because they have invited God's wrath through unforgiveness. Don't incur God's wrath on yourself any more, learn to forgive!

Secondly, unforgiveness hands you over to the tormentors of life. The King in the parable handed over the unforgiving servant to tormentors (Matthew 18:34-35). The tormentors of life could be spiritual, mental or physical.

Another woman was barren and about to undergo an operation when the surgeon, a born-again and Holy Spirit-filled Christian, heard a warning from within. The Holy Spirit ministered to him that the woman would not require surgery, but to merely forgive someone. The surgeon told her what the Holy Spirit ministered to him and asked her who she needed to forgive.

Examining herself, she realised that she was embittered against her brother in-law. As she confessed her unforgiveness, healing came her way, and she testified that she was not only healed, but also blessed with a baby!

If the many things that bother people today are traced, we will discover that they are caused by unforgiveness. At one of our Women conventions, a sister, on hearing the devastating effects of unforgiveness, immediately forgave someone she had for some years vowed never to forgive. To her utter surprise, a mysterious disease she had been carrying in her body for many years disappeared totally.

"I won't forgive you" is a deadly statement. Parents need to forgive their children and children their parents. That's how to make your home glorious. The tormentors of poverty, sickness, barrenness, failure, confusion, etc are dealing with many families today and robbing them because of unforgiveness. Your family must be free!.

Unforgiveness also leads to **tension** in the home, and God does not come down except in the cool of the day. This means He only comes when your home is cool. You cannot enjoy fellowship with God in a family where there is unforgiveness. No matter how much you pray or study the Word of God, the heaven over your head will be very hard and impenetrable. This can be very disastrous!.

Also, unforgiveness is a **seed**. The type of seed you sow determines what you will harvest (Genesis 8:22). If you live in unforgiveness, God won't forgive you either (Matthew 6:14-15). Except you are forgiven, there is no hope of heaven for you. So, your refusal to forgive others robs you of being forgiven by God, and you may end up regretting it.

Combating Unforgiveness

By Confession

The first person to confess to is God. Unforgiveness is a sin and it breaks your fellowship with God. Then, you need to approach your spouse or whoever is concerned in love, discussing your grievance, listening to his/her explanation and giving room for apology. If you are the offender, learn to say "sorry".

Thereafter, let the matter end at that point. It shouldn't be a subject of discussion between you and other people or friends anymore.

> *Confess your faults one to another...*
>
> James 5:16

> *Moreover if thy brother shall trespass against thee, go and tell him his fault between thee and him alone...*
>
> Matthew 18:15

Then Forget

> *...Forgetting those things that are behind and reaching forth unto those things which are before.*
>
> Philippians 3:13

Once a matter has been settled, let it remain settled! You must forgive and forget. Whenever past hurts resurface, plead the Blood of Jesus against them and keep reaching forth for the better things ahead.

Think Right

> *For from within, out of the heart of men, proceed evil thoughts...*
>
> Mark 7:21

Think right about people, especially your spouse and family members, even if and when they offend you. One thing my husband does, which I have learnt from him, is to make excuses for the people who offend him. He says, "Maybe it's the best he knows to do." Learn to make allowances for other people's mistakes. Even if the offence is deliberate, let God be the judge (Psalm94:1).

Speak Right

You can live without hurting your partner by guarding your tongue, choosing your words carefully and speaking wisely (Proverbs 25:11). If you have offended your partner, saying "I am sorry" from the depth of your heart, is not asking for too much. You must get into the habit of apologizing, owning up when you are wrong.

One major way to speak right is to be quick to hear, slow to speak, and slow to wrath.

Act Right

You must be prepared to keep quiet when your partner is talking. Let your actions portray forgiveness and love all the time. Forgiveness paralyses the activities of the devil in your family.

14

An Answer To Separation

And I will restore to you the years that the locust hath eaten...

Joel 2:25

Restoration means to bring something or somebody back to a former place or position. This implies a return to an original position, back to how it was at the beginning.

Many people are today in situations and conditions that make them shed secret tears. They have tasted the joy of union with a life partner and then suddenly the story changes. Their joy is turned to sorrow, their pleasure to pain, and fun to frustration. Suddenly, it seems there's no way out. Thank God there is a way out of such pains and sorrows in Christ Jesus. God is a God of restoration.

Divorce

Divorce means legally ending a marriage. It occurs when a couple begins to see themselves as incompatible and decide that they can no longer live with each other as husband and wife. Their interest in each other dies or turns to someone else.

What does the Word of God say about divorce?

> *Yet ye say, Wherefore? Because the Lord hath been witness between thee and the wife of thy youth, against whom thou hast dealt treacherously: yet is she thy companion, and the wife of thy covenant.*
>
> *And did not he make one? Yet had he the residue of the spirit. And wherefore one? That he might seek a godly seed. Therefore take heed to your spirit, and let none deal treacherously against the wife of his youth.*
>
> *For the Lord, the God of Israel, saith that he hateth putting away: for one covereth violence with his garment, saith the Lord of hosts: therefore take heed to your spirit, that ye deal not treacherously.*
>
> *Malachi 2:14-16*

God hates putting away, divorce, and every violent act against one's spouse in marriage. Since marriage is a covenant for life, divorce should never be considered as an option to settle problems in marriage. God's Word is more than enough to handle any problem in your marriage, home and in any area of your life.

The Pharisees asked Jesus:

> *...Is it lawful for a man to put away his wife for every cause?*
>
> *And he answered...Moses because of the hardness of your hearts suffered you to put away your wives: but from the beginning it was not so.*
>
> *...What therefore God hath joined together, let not man put asunder.*
>
> Matthew 19:3-8

From the beginning, God's intention was for man and his wife to be together for life. He put into both the ability to accommodate, support and complement each other.

But trying to run marriage without God has brought undue conflicts into homes. When you acknowledge God, giving His Word pre-eminence and allowing it to guide you, the mention of the word "divorce" will be far from you.

If you are not yet divorced, but are at the verge of it, please understand that God hates divorce. Don't give up on your marriage. This testimony will bless you and show you that there is still hope for you.

"I came to Word of Faith Bible Institute (WOFBI) to strengthen my faith, to enable me deal with life issues,

especially building a happy family life, successful business and strong Christian family.

Before then, I went through marital woes with my wife, especially after I lost my job, to the point that I contemplated divorcing her. But on listening to your teaching about breaking the marriage covenant, I decided to desist from this action and seek more counsel".

The Way Out

Jesus told a parable someday, about a householder who sowed good seeds in his field, but awoke to find tares growing alongside the good seeds. When asked how this was possible, considering that he had sown only good seeds, the householder replied:

> *...An enemy hath done this...*
>
> Matthew 13:28

A sweet marriage is like the good seed sown by the householder. But when a couple is spiritually asleep, the enemy creeps in and sows seeds of discord, disunity, hatred and bitterness. The enemy magnifies every small issue until things are out of control.

A proverb says, "Tall oaks from little acorns grow." Problems in marriages that have grown so big and tall started as tiny seeds. To solve some of these problems, you must trace them to their roots, and find out how and where you missed it and pull them out from the roots. When this is done, you must accept responsibility for your actions and reactions and admit these before God in prayer. Don't shift blame. If you do, you are only trying to exonerate yourself and restoration cannot come that way.

Forgiveness is the next step. When you consider all that God has forgiven you of, you will be wicked to refuse to forgive your spouse of any wrong he or she must have done to you.

There is nothing your spouse has done that cannot be forgiven. Even when you feel betrayed and let down, God's grace is available to help you put the past behind. The Bible instructs you to be tender- hearted, ready to forgive even as God has forgiven you (Ephesians 4:32).

In addition, if you have truly forgiven, plead the blood of Jesus to purge out bitterness, hatred and the likes. When memories of those past faults come to your mind, plead the blood of Jesus.

Then again, when your heart is free of evil, fill it up with all that is good, true, lovely, of good report, praise worthy and pure (Philippians 4:8). Your words must reflect the new state of your heart. Speak good of your spouse, encourage and praise him or her. Even if he or she is not immediately transformed, keep speaking positively, until you see a change.

Let your actions correspond with your thoughts and speech. Let your countenance mirror your heart, and healing will come to your home. Choose to give thanks, not "for" your situation, but "in" it, because that unhealthy situation is temporal; it will soon change (Acts 16:25-26).

The consequences of divorce are very distasteful. Do all you can to avoid it. Only those who have experienced it can tell of its attendant pains. It is comparable to amputation. Just as there is physical amputation, the same way divorce can be likened to marital amputation. It should never be encouraged. Someone shared this testimony recently:

"My aunty's husband left about two years ago; without any quarrel, he just left her with two children. When the Bishop was praying for restoration of broken homes on Wednesday, I wrote my aunty's name and her husband's and believed God for a restoration. I went there today and saw that the man was back home! I asked him when he made up his mind to come back and he said Wednesday evening (the very time the Bishop was praying)!"

The same God who did this for them can intervene in your situation also. Believe!

Divorced? What Next?

Perhaps you are already divorced. "What next?," you may ask! The Bible says:

> *Shake thyself from the dust; arise, and sit down, O Jerusalem: loose thyself from the bands of thy neck, O captive daughter of Zion.*
>
> Isaiah 52:2

If you are already divorced, you can arise from the dust where you are sitting and stop bemoaning your situation. Shake off the dust of self-justification, bitterness or anger. Arise in the study of the Word and in prayer. Do away with restlessness, worry or anxiety. Rather than worry about how you will cope with the situation, submit all to God in prayer and take your rest (Philippians 4:6).

All hope is not lost yet! God is a God of a second chance. By following God's instructions, that broken relationship can be mended. If He could restore life to Lazarus after four days in the grave, then He can cause your home to come back to life. By believing, you trigger off the miraculous. Martha wanted help for Lazarus before he died but when he died, she did not believe Jesus could raise him up (John 11:1-44). Before a problem "dies" we believe it can be raised, but after it appears dead we write it off. Don't write off your marriage and home, Jesus is still able to bring it back to life. Someone shared this testimony in church:

"Today marks three years since I started attending this church. What brought me here was my spiritual lack, not material lack. I was born again five years before I came here and was attending a living church.

Since I started worshipping here, God has given me the spirit of understanding ofthe Word of God and my faith has been on the increase. Most importantly, there has been captivity turn around in my life, particularly in my marriage.

My marriage technically broke down on the wedding day, at the reception table! But I stayed on in it for almost a decade. It was a thorn in the flesh. Eventually, I had to leave. From right inside my matrimonial home, I got a SAN to prosecute the divorce.

*I got born again after then, but the Word never came to me until I got to this church. There was a teaching on forgiveness one day, which made me realise that I had been living in self-righteousness all along. I forgive, but don't forget. I got this corrected in my mind and through the anointed book, **Marriage Covenant**, and through anointed preachings of the men of God and counselling, my marriage was miraculously healed, and right now, I'm having a honeymoon."*

Perhaps you are divorced already and now you are asking whether re-marriage is possible, particularly in a case where your partner has refused reconciliation. The Bible says:

Yet if the unbelieving one leaves, let him leave; the brother or the sister is not under bondage in such cases, but God has called us to peace.

1 Corinthians 7:15 (NASB)

The Bible says, "**...The brother or sister is not under bondage in such cases...**" The issue of re-marriage can be considered because verse 9 in the Amplified Bible says:

But if they have not self-control (restraint of their passions) they should marry. For it is better to marry than to be aflame (with passion and tortured continually with ungratified desire).But if they have not self-control (restraint of their passions) they should marry. For it is better to marry than to be aflame (with passion and tortured continually with ungratified desire).

But God has called us to peace and not to confusion, so ensure you give peace a chance in whatever steps you take. Let everything be done decently and in order. If your one-time spouse refuses a re-union, then you are free to re-marry, according to scriptures; but only in the Lord. That is, as a believer, your are only permitted to remarry a fellow Christian.

A Word For Single Parents

Having children without the intention of being married is unscriptural, no matter how acceptable it is to the society. Children need the presence of both father and mother. They also need the stability a marriage offers, physically, emotionally, mentally and spiritually. God's Word only allows that children should come from marriage and not between a man in the beer parlour and a lady on the road. Marriage is the proper foundation for raising children. Every child should be brought up in a family setting.

Raising children is real work. That is why God designed that both parents share this responsibility. When one party is not there for any unavoidable reasons, the single parent can hook up to God and let Him fill in the vacuum.

A father of the fatherless, and a judge of the widows, is God in his holy habitation.

God setteth the solitary in families: he bringeth out those which are bound with chains: but the rebellious dwell in a dry land.

Psalm 68:5-6

A Word To The Widow/Widower

Widowhood is painful! No one wants to think about it, let alone read an article about it. One may have felt forcefully stripped of the honour, pleasure and joy of marriage. However, God Who is a restorer can restore any honour lost in marriage through widowhood. The good news is that not only can He restore such honour, but He is willing and can do so right now.

> *The wife is bound by the law as long as her husband liveth; but if her husband be dead, she is at liberty to be married to whom she will, only in the Lord.*
>
> 1 Corinthians 7:39

It is appropriate to mention here that re-marriage is in line with God's Word, if a widow or widower so desires (1 Timothy 5:14). Are you a widow or widower? You are scripturally permitted to marry only a born-again child of God. Here is a testimony that will bless you:

After being widowed, a particular lady, quite advanced in age, was invited to the church by a member of the church. On hearing the Word of God, she was lifted out of her depression and decided to give her life to Christ and forget the pains of being widowed and her bitterness towards God.

After getting born again, she was encouraged to keep fellowshipping in church, rather than mourning. She soon discovered it was possible to marry again. On one of those fellowship days, she met with the Bishop and indicated her desire to remarry, but also confessed her anxiety of not believing she would find a suitable born-again believer who's her age. She was rebuked of her lack of faith and prayed for, for favour. She is now happily married to a caring believer and enjoying the honour in marriage such as she didn't enjoy in her first marriage!

Praise God, He is a God of restoration! If you are widowed, yours shall be the next testimony.

I believe you have been mightily blessed by this book. Right now, as I pray for your family, believe God for a unique touch in your home. You will have a testimony!

In the name of Jesus, I ask for the hand of God to rest heavily on your home. Because marriage is good and honourable, I declare that from today, you begin to enjoy God's goodness and honour in your home. In whatever area you believe God for a touch or a miracle, I command a release of the same, in the name of Jesus.

If you are single and desiring a life partner, right now, I pronounce your partner found and your home established, in the name of Jesus.

If you are married and going through turbulent times, I say "Peace be still" to every storm in your home. Wherever there has been a satanic obstacle, by the anointing of the Holy Spirit, I declare all such yokes broken and destroyed, never to resurface again.

If you are barren, I curse that curse of barrenness.

Because God has declared you fruitful, you cannot be barren. Whatever the enemy has stolen, I declare it found and replaced. Whatever has not been functioning properly in your body, I command it to begin to work. You are free, in Jesus' name!

I expect your testimonies. Jesus' is Lord!

15

Proofs Of Restoration

MARRIAGE RESTORED!

"A husband and wife who had travelled all the way to their village for the dissolution of their marriage, for some reasons changed their minds and returned home to get a legal divorce first. While at home, someone invited them to one of our women's programmes.

After listening to the anointed message, both man and wife agreed to have a second go at their marriage. They re-exchanged wedding vows and rekindled the fire of love and commitment." - **Living Faith Women Fellowship, Makurdi**

THERE IS NOW PEACE IN MY HOME!

"After my first child in May, 1981, I went from church

to church in search of another child, not really knowing the Word of God. I was anxious, desperate, worried and lacked good relationship with people. This almost caused me my marriage.

However, I got another baby in December, 1991 (10 years later), and I thought peace had come to the home. But no! I started coming to this church in July, 1994 and gave my life to Christ in October, 1994.

I started hearing the Word of God in a different way, in a way I had never heard it before! I started seeing changes in my home and in the relationship between my husband and I. Peace, joy, harmony and great love were restored to me.

Again, I became anxious for another child, since my baby was now over four years old. I read your book, You Can Overcome Anxiety, and anxiety died in me, because I now know God is able to do all things.

My husband, by His grace, is now a man, husband and father. There is now peace in my home and office and m y relation with other people is excellent." - *Hart, C. I.*

HUSBAND SAVED AND TONGUE-TALKING!

"When we started preparing for the WMI convention, I prayed to God and told Him I wanted my own family renewed. I did not like the names I was being called (I was being called the wife of an unbeliever) and told God I didn't want to be called that again.

God did a great thing! Even before the convention began, God changed my husband! On the day of the last Breakthrough Night, my husband said we must go to church. We came to church together and he gave his life to Christ that day. He has now stopped smoking and everything has changed in his life. He is now a new born person!

During the convention, on the day of the anointing service, I did not have a handkerchief with me when mantles were being blessed. Just at that moment, the chain I had on my neck fell on my laps and I picked it and raised it up when I heard God say, 'Use it'.

On getting home, I placed the chain on my husband's neck and placed my anointed forehead on his and he started speaking in tongues! My husband had always criticised speaking in tongues, and here he was doing just that!" - **Efemuaye, L.**

'...MY HUSBAND CHANGED!'

"I married my husband by proxy and living together was very strenuous. God kept me there anyhow, but I was not comfortable, as I suffered various hurts. At the convention in December, I attended the seminar (Marital Bliss), where the Bishop's wife ministered. When it was time for prayers, she joined the prayers at my side. She prayed that all that had sustained hurts in their marriages should receive their healings.

The second day, I met her in the corridor and she strangely put her hand on my shoulder like an old friend. I say 'strange' because I am not in 'close circuit' with her.

From that very moment, I found myself thinking about my husband and I felt relaxed. I could then call him 'my husband' without any inhibitions or second thought.

Strangely, he too changed. He started telling me that my food was delicious and whenever he came home, he would buy something for me. This he had not done for over 15 to 16 years. Whenever I wanted to manage the soup, he says 'No!' and provides money for another soup.I give all the glory to God." - **Ajanaku, A. O.**

'IT'S LIKE I'M WEDDED ANEW!'

"I've been married for over 12 years now and what I'm enjoying now, I've never enjoyed since I got married.

I thank God for our mother in the Lord, who during the Family Renewal Seminar in March 1995 preached to us. Ever since, the Lord has turned around the tide, *just through my obedience to the Word.*

She laid emphasis on wives being submissive to their husbands in everything, just like the Church submits to Christ. She also said we were to be submissive in everything. I didn't realise that I wasn't totally submissive to my husband. I wept so much in church that day and went to the Lord saying, 'Lord, from this day, I know that obedience is the key.'

Ever since, I've been enjoying what all my fasting, binding and all couldn't deliver to me. I had done so many things to get my husband to love me—fasted, bound, loosed —but I thank God that now it's like I'm wedded anew.

Just yesterday morning, to confirm God's faithfulness in my home, my husband gave me a cheque of one hundred thousand naira, which I have cashed this morning. I now enjoy peace, love and harmony." - **Adebayo, L.**

BARRENNESS IS BROKEN!

"I have been married for seven years. Shortly after my wedding, my period ceased. Thinking I was pregnant I kept expecting my baby. It turned out that it was a false alarm. From the results of an ultrasound scan, I was referred to the doctor, who said I had a small uterus, too

small to accommodate a baby. I laughed it off, reasoning that if God has given those without wombs children, I who has one, has hope.

*At the last convention (June, 1994) I got up when my case was described by Pastor Mrs. Faith Oyedepo. Immediately after prayers, my period was restored, and in July, I became pregnant! My baby was born this April and is named David!" - **Asubiojo, M.***

20 YEARS BARRENNESS SHATTERED!

"During the Maiduguri Women Zonal Convention in April, Pastor (Mrs.) Faith Oyedepo instructed that those who are yet to have children should come to the meeting with baby things. I came along to the service with two baby bibs. I had two sisters and a brother in the south, who after their marriages for some time now still have no children and I decided to stand in for them.

*My elder brother's case was worse — he had been married for 20 years. But to the glory of God, in July 1995 (three months after the Convention), I got a letter informing me that my two sisters and my brother's wife were all pregnant!" - **Okani, M.***

References

1. **"Two Shall Be One"**

    C. M. Ward

2. Ibid.

3. **Arise, Daughters Of Sarah, Arise**

H. Ramaya

4. **Afraid No More**

    H. Norman Wright

5. Ibid.

The Author

Faith Abiola Oyedepo has through the leading of the Holy Spirit, brought hope, joy, peace and life into many families and homes in her generation.

For many years that she received the ministry for families and homes, she has in no little measure dedicated her entire life to showing people the perfect will of God concerning their family relationships and homes. Her regular and scintillating weekly newspaper and internet columns - Family Matters, Family Success and Family Life, among others - have helped in no small way in achieving this goal.

Also, she is reaching out to the less privileged, the needy and those in the valley of decision, through her Faith Abiola Oyedepo Foundation (FAOF).

She has a divine mandate to make her shoulders available and enrich the lives of singles and unmarried persons in a unique way.

Pastor Faith has written over 20 anointed and impactful books that have transformed many lives and given them a change of story, including her best-selling title: *Rescued From Destruction*.

An anointed preacher of the Gospel, Pastor Faith has been doggedly supportive of her husband [Dr. David O. Oyedepo, the Visionary/President Of Living Faith Church Worldwide Inc.] in the work of the ministry.

They are the parents of four grown children – David Jnr., Isaac, Love and Joys.

Books By The Author

- **Building A Successful Family**
- **Making Marriage Work**
- **Success In Marriage**
  (Co-authored with Dr. David Oyedepo)
- **Marriage Covenant**
- **Raising Godly Children**
- **Rescued From Destruction**
- **Single With A Difference**
- **The Effective Minister's Wife**
- **The Spirit Of Faith**
- **A Living Witness** (Expanded version)
- **Nurturing The Incorruptible Seed** (Expanded version)
- **Service: The Master Key** (Expanded version)
- **The Dignity Of The Believer** (Expanded version)
- **Growing In Grace**
- **The Power Of The Communion Table**
- **Healing, Health And Wholeness**
- **Overcoming Anxiety**
- **Salvation: The Way Of Escape**
- **The Healing Scriptures**
- **The Healing Ministry Of Jesus Christ**
- **You Are Welcome To God's Family**
- **Understanding Motherhood**

INSIDE VIEW OF
Faith Tabernacle

Dr. David Oyedepo is the founding president of the Living Faith Church Worldwide Inc. And senior pastor of the Faith Tabernacle, a 50,000 capacity sanctuary located in Canaan Land, Ota, a suburb of Lagos Nigeria.

The construction of this gigantic architectural masterpiece was completed within twelve months and dedicated on September 18, 1999. Built totally debt free and without any foreign inputs! To God alone be all the glory.

Today, Faith Tabernacle stands as the home of signs and wonders for men and women all over the world who keep coming in droves to worship the King of kings and Lord of lords, Jesus Christ the Son of the Living God.

OUTSIDE VIEW OF FAITH TABERNACLE

CHURCH MASS TRANSIT— Over 250 buses commuting the worshippers to Church from all nook and crannies of Lagos & environs

Visit our website for more information: www.davidoyedepoministries.org

Aerial View Of Covenant University

College of Business & Social Sciences

Covenant University

Dr. David Oyedepo is the visioner and Chancellor of Covenant University founded 21st October 2002. Today, Covenant University has student population of over 6,000, all fully boarded on campus; in a state of the art halls of residence. All degree programmes offered at Covenant University are fully accredited by the appropriate accrediting body. As at date, CU offers 42 degree programmes in 3 different faculties:

COLLEGE OF SCIENCE AND TECHNOLOGY:

Computer Science, Management Information System, Architecture, Building Technology, Estate Management, Industrial Mathematics, Industrial Chemistry, Industrial Physics, Biochemistry, Biology, Microbiology, Computer Engineering, Information and Communication Technology, Electrical and Electronic Engineering, Civil Engineering, Mechanical Engineering, Chemical Engineering, Petroleum Engineering.

COLLEGE OF HUMAN DEVELOPMENT:

Philosophy, Psychology, Counseling, English Language, Mass Communication, Public Relations and Advertising, Sociology and French.

COLLEGE OF BUSINESS AND SOCIAL SCIENCES:

Accounting, Taxation and Public Sector Accounting, Banking and Finance, Business Administration, Marketing, Industrial Relations and Human Resource Management, Economics, Demography and Social Statistics, International Relations, Political Science, Public Administration, Policy and Strategic Studies.

Visit our website for more information: **www.covenantuniversity.com**

More Facilities@ Covenant University

College of Science & Technology

University Library (Centre For Learning Resources)

4,000 Seat Students Chapel

More Facilities@ Covenant University

Post Graduate Building

Senior Staff Residential Quarters

Covenant University 100 Room Ultra Modern Guest House

Students Hall Of Residence

Landmark University

Senate Building

Landmark University is a product of the education mandate given to Dr. David Oyedepo. Dedicated on the 21st of March 2011, it is the second university to be established by his ministry.

The vision of the university is to raise leaders with particular emphasis of promoting agricultural enterprise among others with a learning focus that makes a graduate bread winners, job creators and solution providers

The teaching, research and community service of the university are weaved around the intellectual and natural resource endowment of her immediate community.

Landmark University Offer the following courses:

COLLEGE OF AGRICULTURAL SCIENCES:

General Agriculture, Animal Science, Plant Science, Agricultural Extension & Rural Development, Agricultural Economics.

COLLEGE OF SCIENCE & ENGINEERING:

Industrial Chemistry, Industrial Mathematics, Industrial Physics, Computer Science, Biology, Biochemistry, Microbiology, Electrical And Information Engineering, Mechanical Engineering, Chemical Engineering, Civil Engineering, Agricultural Engineering.

COLLEGE OF BUSINESS & SOCIAL SCIENCES:

Accounting, Banking And Finance, Business Administration, Economics, Sociology, Political Science, International Relations.

More Facilities@ Landmark University

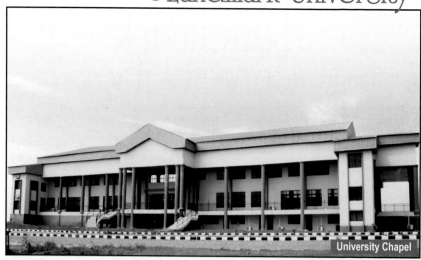

University Chapel

College Building

Cafetaria

More Facilities@ Landmark University

One of the Student's Halls Of Residence

Professors Village

Staff Quarters

370 902 2955